To someone special:

_____

From:

_____

Date:

_____

Words of Jesus

for Girls

Carolyn Larsen

Words of Jesus for Girls

Copyright © 2012 by Christian Art Kids,
an imprint of Christian Art Publishers,
PO Box 1599, Vereeniging, 1930, RSA

359 Longview Drive, Bloomingdale, IL 60108, USA

First edition 2012

Designed by Christian Art Kids

Images used under license from Shutterstock.com

Scripture quotations are taken from the *Holy Bible*,
New International Version® NIV®. Copyright © 1973,
1978, 1984, 2011 by International Bible Society.
Used by permission of Zondervan Publishing House.
All rights reserved.

Scripture quotations marked NLT are taken from the *Holy Bible*,
New Living Translation®, second edition. Copyright © 1996,
2004 by Tyndale House Publishers, Inc., Carol Stream, Illinois 60188.
All rights reserved.

Set in 11 on 14 pt Avenir LT Std by Christian Art Kids

Printed in China

ISBN 978-1-4321-0131-2

13 14 15 16 17 18 19 20 21 22 – 12 11 10 9 8 7 6 5 4 3

Dedication

I wish to dedicate this book
to a very special young lady.
McKenna Liebenow and her mother, Cathy,
helped me to reconnect with the challenges
and joys of being a young girl these days.
I appreciate McKenna's insight and honesty.
Bless you, McKenna, as you continue
to know Christ better, grow in your
faith and use the wonderful talents He
has given you in service back to Him.

January

Getting Along with Others

It's a pretty simple command, right? Treat other people the way you want them to treat you. Yeah, Jesus' words are straightforward.

In fact, this is called the Golden Rule of how to get along with others. But, Jesus didn't speak these words as instructions on getting along with your friends only. This command came in the middle of instructions on how to treat people you don't really like; in other words, your enemies.

It's not easy to treat an enemy kindly, but it is the Jesus-thing to do.

Living It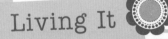

Maggie has been telling lies about Kelly – spreading rumors that she cheats on tests. Maggie has even posted that kind of stuff online.

What Kelly might want to do is tell lies about Maggie. You know, get even. But, Jesus says not to. In fact, He says to do the opposite. Jesus says to say nice things about Maggie or nothing at all. Treating Maggie with kindness might make her think about how she is treating Kelly. It's what Jesus would do!

What's Really Important?

Wow, Jesus has a way of cutting through all the garbage that the world feeds us as to what's really important, doesn't He?

The Internet, TV, magazines, even some friends and teachers claim that being successful means being super beautiful, making lots of money, having power, and being important.

Jesus says there is something more important – taking care of your soul. *What's* He saying? Success is making sure you have accepted Jesus as Savior and that you obey His teachings every day.

Success is living for Jesus, loving Him and loving others.

> "What good is it for someone to gain the whole world, and yet lose or forfeit their very self?"
> Luke 9:25

Living It

The most important thing to Linnie is winning the election for class president. For her, that means success because she wants the power and the recognition of being in charge of her class. She is so focused on the election that she has stopped reading her Bible, stopped praying (for anything except the victory) and has even stopped spending time with her friends.

Becoming president is more important to her than being close to Jesus. Her priorities are turned upside down. She has lost sight of what's really important – knowing and serving Jesus.

Look in the Mirror, Girl!

"Why worry about a speck in your friend's eye when you have a log in your own?"

Matthew 7:3 NLT

Many times the things we criticize in other people are the very things we struggle with ourselves. That's why Jesus said, "Hey, pay attention to your own struggles before you criticize someone else."

It's easier to pick on someone else for their bad behavior than it is to deal with your own problems, but that's the wrong thing to do. The truth is that everyone sins. Everyone makes bad choices.

Take care of your own sins before you criticize someone else for theirs.

Living It

Delia is negative. Seriously negative. She can find something bad to say about nearly every person or situation. The weird thing is that she criticizes other people for being negative. "Cindy is always complaining. She finds the bad in anything," Delia says.

Well, if Delia takes Jesus' words to heart, she will fix her own problem before criticizing someone else. It's not easy, but it's the right thing to do!

Secret Giving!

Newsflash! Doing things to help the needy is not all about you! Sure, it's nice to get a thank you or a pat on the back, but that should not be the only reason you give to or help others.

You should help others because Jesus says to love others. Do your good deeds in secret so no one knows what you did except you and God. It's a great feeling to help.

God will take care of the pat on the back. No worries.

> "When you give to the needy, do not let your left hand know what your right hand is doing, so that your giving may be in secret."
> Matthew 6:3-4

Living It

Andie works in the food pantry. She babysits children during refugee classes. She gives money to help the poor. She is super generous and everyone knows it because she tells everyone.

Most of her friends just walk away when she starts talking about all her good deeds. They don't compliment or admire her. They get really tired of her bragging.

Andie must have missed Jesus' message: "Do good things, but be quiet about it!"

The Good News

> "For God so loved the world that He gave His one and only Son, that whoever believes in Him shall not perish but have eternal life."
>
> John 3:16

Jesus spoke this famous Scripture verse about Himself as He was explaining salvation to Nicodemus. God loves you so much that He sent His only Son from heaven to earth. He wouldn't be received here as a king. He would be criticized, persecuted and eventually murdered.

But, here's the deal — He knew that was going to happen. God knew it, too.

They agreed to the plan because they love you and wanted to make a way for your sins to be forgiven so you could know God personally.

Cool, eh?

Living It

Cady has been to church a gazillion times (that's what she says) because her parents make her go every week. But, she writes notes during the sermon. She daydreams during the worship time.

She doesn't really listen to the message of how much God loves her and that Jesus died for her sins. Too bad. She can't really know God until she hears and believes!

Humility Wins!

Pride will get you nowhere with Jesus. Nope, He makes it very clear that the most important people from His viewpoint are those who serve others, not those who brag about how wonderful they are.

So, wanting to be Number One and bragging about how important you are or only being friends with others if they can do something for you is not good.

Don't brag. Don't be full of pride. Do stuff for others and help others step into the spotlight. That's a Jesus-person!

"Anyone who wants to be first must be the very last, and the servant of all."
Mark 9:35

Living It

Braggin' Bekah. That's what Bekah's friends call her behind her back. No, that isn't nice, but they get tired of her constantly bragging about how pretty, smart and good at everything she is. When one of them tells a story she always has to tell a better one and make herself look more important.

If Bekah learned from Jesus' words she would know that the best way to be Number One is to be the last one of all. Humility wins. Pride loses.

Settle Things Privately

> "If another believer sins against you, go privately and point out the offense."
> Matthew 18:15 NLT

Big problems develop when you go public about a mean thing someone has done to you. That makes all your other friends choose sides. Often, half of your friends get mad at you and half at the other person.

It's really bad. That's why Jesus said to go talk privately with someone who has hurt you or done something wrong.

Settle it privately because it is better for the family of God.

Living It

Lizzie told an outright lie about Megan who found out about it from another friend. Now, Megan could go to all her friends and tell them what Lizzie did.

She could do her best to get them all to agree with her that what Lizzie did was really creepy and they should not be her friend anymore. Except, Jesus said that first she should try talking to Lizzie alone. She should see if they can settle their problem privately so that a lot of other people don't get mad at Lizzie, too.

A Clean, Pure Heart

This Scripture verse is in a section of Matthew known as the Beatitudes. They are comforting verses about people who find favor with Jesus.

What does it mean to be pure in heart? Something is pure only after it has been washed, because only then it is clean.

A pure heart is free of sin and is focused on loving and serving God. It has no self-centeredness, no critical spirit, but has complete trust in God.

> "Blessed are the pure in heart, for they will see God."
> Matthew 5:8

Living It

Jenny says she loves God. She goes to church and reads her Bible and prays. Everyone thinks she is serious about her faith. But, they can't see what's in Jenny's heart. God can, though. He knows that she only cares about Him on Sundays. She is good at putting on a show for the rest of the week.

However, Jenny will find out one day that she isn't fooling God and that she can't honestly obey any other commands if her heart hasn't been cleaned of its sins (self-centeredness) so that it can be pure.

The Good Doctor

"It is not the healthy who need a doctor, but the sick. I have not come to call the righteous, but sinners."

Mark 2:17

Jesus is the only one who can cure the sickness of sin. That's why He didn't just hang out in the temple all the time. He made sure He was around people who didn't know Him.

For you, that means it's OK to have friends who don't go to church. Of course, you have to be careful that they don't pull you into doing things that are disobedient to God. You can be a positive influence by telling them about Jesus and living out your faith in front of them!

Living It

Mallory is a gymnast on a club team. She loves learning new skills and competing. But, she also loves that there are girls on the team who don't know Jesus.

Mal isn't pushy about preaching to them. But, they know she is a Christian and she shows love and kindness to others. Once in a while someone even asks her to pray for them. Mal is living out her faith in front of those who don't know Jesus!

God Alone

You've heard the saying, "He's playing with your mind." It means someone is messing with your thinking about what is right and wrong. That's what Satan did when he tempted Jesus.

Satan tried to get Jesus to worship him instead of God. He did that by waiting until Jesus was really hungry, then offering to turn stones into bread … if Jesus would worship him. Jesus had an answer, though – "worship and serve God alone!"

That was right for Jesus and it is right for you!

> Jesus answered, "It is written: 'Worship the Lord your God and serve Him only.'"
> Luke 4:8

Living It

If you ask Mara if she worships God alone, she will say yes, with no doubt in her mind. However, she isn't being honest with herself. Mara does worship God, but she also "worships" her friends.

Maybe this sounds crazy to you, but when your friends' opinions matter more to you than what God thinks, then your focus of worship is messed up. Mara needs to get her priorities straight – God first, friends somewhere down the line.

Trusting God

> "Do not let your hearts be troubled. Trust in God, and trust also in Me."
>
> John 14:1 NLT

Have you ever been so worried that you have a knot in the pit of your stomach? It's an awful feeling. The crazy thing is that this usually happens when you're worried about something you can't do anything about.

What's cool is that Jesus knows that those times happen in our lives and He has an answer – instead of worrying, trust Him. Yep, tell Him what you're worried about and let Him handle it.

He will. You can trust Him.

Living It

Krissy's mom and dad fight constantly – like major shouting matches. Krissy worries that they will split up and then some days she worries that they won't and life will always be like this.

She worries about what will happen to her if they do separate. She can't fix this problem. It's too big. The best thing she can do is to tell God about it, ask Him to handle it and to take care of what happens to her. Then, trust Him to do those things.

First Things First

Relationships are important to Jesus. They are more important than pretty much anything else except our salvation. So, Jesus says, "Don't bother praying and asking God for anything if you are holding a grudge against someone."

First things first. Forgive the person you are mad at before asking God for anything. Forgive those who hurt you just as God forgives you for hurting Him.

> "When you stand praying, if you hold anything against anyone, forgive them, so that your Father in heaven may forgive you."
>
> Mark 11:25

Living It

Sara is trying to say her nightly prayer just like she does every night. But something is in the way. She is so mad at her friend Elaina that all her prayers ask God to make Elaina pay for the way she hurt Sara. Not good.

Sara needs to forgive her friend and if she isn't able to, she can ask God to help her with that. After she forgives her friend, then she can actually pray and know that God will forgive her sins and answer her prayers.

Light in the Darkness

> "I am the light of the world. Whoever follows Me will never walk in darkness, but will have the light of life."
>
> John 8:12

Evil is often compared with darkness. You never see scary, bad places in the movies shown as bright and sunny. Darkness can be scary, especially when you can't see where you're going and you don't know what's ahead of you. But, Jesus is the Light of the world.

So, if you stay in close touch with Him by praying and reading His Word, you will never be in darkness. Jesus is always with you and His light fills the darkness. Then, even though you encounter hardship, you are never alone.

Living It

Lizzie's world is very dark. Her mom has been really sick for a long time and things are not looking good for her health. Lizzie got scared about everything and started hanging out with kids who don't make good choices.

Slowly she sank into their world and now does things that are not pleasing to God – and she knows it. Lizzie needs to turn to Jesus. The light of His love will show Lizzie a better way to live and will fill the darkness of the fear she lives in.

Knowing His Voice

Jesus is the Great Shepherd and we are His sheep. A shepherd leads his flock to food and water. He protects them from wild animals.

Those are the things Jesus does for us. He protects us and cares for us. One cool thing is that sheep learn to recognize their own shepherd's voice. So, when he calls they go to him. If they hear another shepherd call, they don't respond.

Learn to recognize the Great Shepherd's voice and listen only to Him.

> "The sheep listen to his voice. His sheep follow him because they know his voice."
> John 10:4

Living It

Lucy listens to whatever voice is in her ear. So, if she is with friends who don't follow Jesus and they want her to do something, she does it, even if it is disobedient to God.

The Great Shepherd's voice doesn't usually yell. It's that quiet little voice in your mind that tells you the right thing to do. Some might even call it your conscience. Lucy needs to learn to recognize the Shepherd's voice and listen to it.

Keep On Loving!

"If someone slaps you on one cheek, turn to them the other also. If someone takes your coat, do not withhold your shirt from them."

Luke 6:29

Have you ever been hurt by someone and your immediate desire is to hurt back – even more than the person hurt you?

Jesus says, "Don't do that." In fact, He says, "Turn the other cheek, in other words, give the person the chance to hurt you again."

Why would He say this? Because loving others is very important to Jesus. Don't go for revenge – let Him take care of those who hurt you – you just love and love and love.

Living It

Denise doesn't like Linda. It's not like she tries to hide it. Denise pushes Linda out of line at the water fountain. She talks loudly about how dumb Linda is, making fun of her clothes, hairstyle and grades.

Linda could try to get even. But, she doesn't. She follows Jesus' command and just keeps on loving Denise. Someday, though it may not be for a while, someday that love will get through to Denise.

Salty Flavors

When salt is used in the preparation of food you can tell by the way it flavors the food. But if salt is spoiled and has lost its flavor, it is useless.

Jesus said His followers are like salt. We flavor the world around us by living out Jesus' love and values to others. We make a difference.

But, if we stop living for Jesus, we lose our usefulness and are no help to His work on earth.

> "You are the salt of the earth. But if the salt loses its saltiness, how can it be made salty again? It is no longer good for anything, except to be thrown out and trampled underfoot."
>
> Matthew 5:13

Living It

Carol's friends know that she's a Christian. They know that she doesn't go to church just to write notes to her friends during the service. She listens. She learns. She reads her Bible and prays during the week. She tries to obey Jesus' teachings.

Because they know these things about Carol, her friends are careful about the jokes they tell, the words they use and the things they do when she is around. Having Carol around "flavors" their world and they know it's because she loves Jesus.

Alive Forever!

"I am the resurrection and the life. The one who believes in Me will live, even though they die; and whoever lives by believing in Me will never die."

John 11:25-26

Everyone is going to die. Death is part of life ... a sad part, but part of it nonetheless. But an important part of the Christian faith is the belief that God has power over death.

The Bible gives many examples of Jesus raising dead people back to life. God raised Jesus back to life when He was murdered. Jesus promises His children that even after we die on this earth, we will live again in heaven with Him forever!

Living It

Christy's beloved grandmother just died and Christy will miss her so much. They spent a lot of time together and enjoyed doing the same things. Christy knows that life will be different, because she won't see her grandmother every day.

But, because she knows Jesus and her grandmother did, too, Christy knows that they will be together again in heaven one day – alive together forever. Jesus promised!

Love the Lord

Jesus says this is the greatest commandment. If Jesus says that, then there is no doubt that it's important. Read this verse over again.

There is no wiggle room for something to be more important or even as important to you as God. Give Him all your heart, soul, mind and strength. Obeying and serving Him should be foremost in your mind.

Let God's love flow through you so completely that you always show love to others. Love is the most basic and important of all the commands of Scripture.

> "Love the Lord your God with all your heart and with all your soul and with all your mind and with all your strength."
> Mark 12:30

Living It

There is something about Lorie that stands out. Everyone notices it. She is just so nice. She is kind and caring. She doesn't say bad things about others. She is always willing to help. She doesn't lose her temper. Lorie is nice.

The reason Lorie stands out is that she loves God with all her heart, in fact with her whole being. She loves God and that love flows through her. It shows to everyone.

Loving Others

> "The second is this: 'Love your neighbor as yourself.' There is no commandment greater than these."
>
> Mark 12:31

Earlier you read about the greatest commandment. This one goes with it: Love your neighbor. These go together because if you love God with all your heart, soul, mind and strength, you can't help but love your neighbor, too.

Love flows through you. You will think about others and what is best for them before you think about yourself and what you want.

This is revolutionary to what the world says!

Living It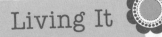

Kate is super excited about sleeping over at Cindy's house on Friday night. They have planned a fun night of painting their nails, eating pizza, watching movies and talking all night. But, when Lisa calls and sadly tells Kate that her new puppy just died, Kate has to reconsider. She can hear the sorrow in Lisa's voice and she knows that she needs to be there for her friend.

Cindy will understand, because she also has a puppy. So, Kate changes the plans she was so excited about so that she can be a comfort to Lisa. She is loving Lisa – more than herself.

God Can Do Anything!

Jesus said this in the middle of a conversation about how hard it is for people to reach heaven.

The truth is that if it were left up to humans, it would not be possible to make a way for people to go to heaven. But, God is the Creator of everything. He can do anything!

So, since God wanted to make a way for people to go to heaven, He did it. Nothing is too hard for God!

> "With man this is impossible, but with God all things are possible."
> Matthew 19:26

Living It

Debbie gets great comfort from Jesus' statement that all things are possible for God. Her life is not the greatest. Her mom is all she has and life is pretty hard for them.

Of course, Debbie is thrilled to know that someday she can live in heaven with God. That's an awesome promise. But, she is also glad to know that nothing that might happen here on earth is bigger than God. He can handle anything!

God Cares

"If that is how God clothes the grass of the field, which is here today, and tomorrow is thrown into the fire, how much more will He clothe you."

Luke 12:28

Terrible things happen around the world – earthquakes, hurricanes, tsunamis, floods. Maybe you are facing some tough things yourself.

Does God not care? Of course, He does, but He doesn't take away the problems. He doesn't leave us to go through them alone either. God cares a lot more for His children than He does about grass and we see that He makes the grass beautifully green.

Trust Him to be with you regardless of how tough life is. He will. He loves you.

Living It

Angie's life is tough. Her dad left. Her mom can't keep a job. Most of the time Angie is left to take care of her brother and herself because her mom stays out late. It's pretty stinky.

But, Angie can be sure that God knows what she is going through. He may not solve her actual problems, but He is with her every step of the way. She is never alone.

Your Job!

God says many times in Scripture that His greatest desire is that everyone who lives would come to know Him.

God wants everyone to be saved. One way that can happen is for the people who do know Him to tell others. Jesus said to go and tell everyone the good news of His love and His plan for salvation.

All of us who know Him have been given that command.

> "Go into all the world and preach the Good News to everyone."
>
> Mark 16:15

Living It

So, how does someone your age preach the Good News? You may not feel qualified to preach like your pastor. However, there is one thing you are really good at – being you.

You can obey Jesus' command by being yourself and being a good friend who lets God's love flow through you. Be an example of God to all your friends!

Love One Another

> "This is My command: Love each other."
> John 15:17

Love is Jesus' basic message. He tells us many times to love one another. He even says to love your enemies.

Jesus wanted people to get along. Wow, if everyone obeyed that command, think what a more pleasant world we would live in! There would be no murders, no crime at all. People would help one another and listen to each other – even when they disagreed.

How wonderful would that be? Love each other. Just do it.

Living It

Natalie just moved to a new town. That means she starts a new school where she doesn't know anyone. Kind of scary, eh? Will anyone be nice to her? Will she be able to make friends or will the other kids make fun of her or even ignore her?

That could have happened except for a couple of girls who knew Jesus' command to love others – and obeyed it. Linnie and Mara talked to Natalie on her first day of school! They asked her to lunch with them and then hang out after school! So cool! Jesus' command in action!

Forgiving Others

Jesus knew that it would not always be easy to forgive someone who hurts you, but when someone asked how many times you have to forgive, His answer was, "Over and over and over."

That's what God does. He forgives our sins day after day. So, we should be willing to do the same, especially when a friend apologizes for what she has done.

Forgive and forgive and forgive. That's what love does.

> "If your brother or sister sins against you, rebuke them; and if they repent, forgive them. Even if they sin against you seven times in a day and seven times come back to you and says, 'I repent,' forgive them."
>
> Luke 17:3-4

Living It

Caroline is tired of it – Allie has done it again. She says she will hang out and they make all sorts of plans. Then, at the last minute, Allie changes her mind. She's done it lots of times!

But this time Allie asked Caroline to forgive her. So, Caroline is giving her another chance because that is what Jesus said she should do. Forgive and forgive and forgive.

Peacemakers Are the Best!

> "Blessed are the peacemakers, for they will be called children of God."
>
> Matthew 5:9

Some girls think they are always right, so they argue about everything. They are even critical of others; picking on styles of clothes they wear or how good they do in school or sports. Ugh, this kind of girl is not much fun.

On the flip side is the girl who tries to keep peace between others. She tries to find bridges between people's differences. This kind of girl is what God wants because she shows love to others even if they are not always kind to her.

She is a peacemaker.

Living It

Kimmie's brother and sister fight about **everything**. If he says the sky is blue then she says it is gray. If he wants pizza for lunch then she wants mac 'n' cheese. Seriously, it gets old.

Kimmie tries to be a bridge between them. She tries to block the arguments that start and find ways to keep peace. She goes back and forth between her brother and sister and paves the way to agreements. Kimmie is a peacemaker.

The Proud Go Down

Being full of pride and bragging about yourself gains no respect from anyone. No one believes the stories except the one spouting the words anyway.

The truth is that none of us can do anything if God hadn't given us our abilities. He is the only one who has any right to brag! Being humble and encouraging others to shine is the better way. The humble person will be respected by others and have God's approval.

Be humble. Give God the glory.

> "Those who exalt themselves will be humbled, and those who humble themselves will be exalted."
>
> Matthew 23:12

Living It

Everyone loves Jill because she is fun to be with, kind, full of laughter, really smart, and can sing beautifully. Well, to be truthful, there isn't much that Jill isn't good at.

But, you would never know that by talking with her. She constantly compliments her friends and encourages them to reach for the stars. She celebrates every one of their successes. Jill never brags about herself. In fact, that's probably why everyone loves her. She is humble and the only thing she brags about is her friends!

God's Amazing Care

"Your Father knows what you need before you ask Him."
Matthew 6:8

Prayer is a special privilege you have to talk with the Creator of everything. You can tell Him what you are scared about and what you need and what you hope. You can talk with Him about anything!

God promises to hear your prayers and to answer them with what He knows is best for you. He can see the whole picture of your life and He knows exactly what you need, even before you know it! He loves you very much so you can trust Him to take care of you!

Living It

Lily and Lena were best buddies and were together constantly. When Kyra moved in next door, Lily's mom invited Kyra and her mom over to visit. Kyra was nice, and pretty soon she was hanging out with Lily and Lena, too.

Then Lena's dad got a new job and they moved away! Lily was very sad, but then she realized that God had taken care of her. He gave her another friend, even before she knew that she needed one!

Light Shows Everything!

Jesus is the Light of the world. When you get close to Him, that light shows you the sin in your life. When you are aware of the sin then you can confess it, ask forgiveness for it and change the way you are living.

But, a person who doesn't want to stop doing bad things will not be comfortable being "in the light" or being close to Jesus. She won't want the bad things she does to show – even to her.

> "Everyone who does evil hates the light, and will not come into the light for fear that their deeds will be exposed."
> John 3:20

Living It

Lucy loves Jesus, but she has a friend who doesn't know Him. Jody does bad things and she often hurts other people. Lucy has tried to tell her friend about Jesus, but Jody doesn't want to hear anything about Him. She says she is just fine the way she is.

Jody doesn't want to admit that she does bad things. She knows that Jesus will make her face her bad choices. So, she stays away from the light. Lucy feels bad about that, but she will keep on trying to tell Jody about Jesus.

Life-Giving Water!

"Everyone who drinks this water will be thirsty again, but whoever drinks the water I give them will never thirst. Indeed, the water I give them will become in them a spring of water welling up to eternal life."

John 4:13-14

People are born with a thirst in their hearts to be loved and to matter to someone. They thirst for meaning in their lives.

People try to quench this thirst in many ways. Some think wealth will do it. Some think popularity, a career or even fame will do it. As they get older, some go the route of alcohol or drugs.

Those things might work for a while. But the only thing that will quench that thirst forever is Jesus. He lasts for eternity.

Living It

Maybe wealth, a successful career or fame doesn't mean much at your age. Hopefully the alcohol and drugs route just seems dumb. So, what will make you feel fulfilled in the future?

Even if you achieve your dreams, the feeling of fulfillment will be temporary. That's evident from celebrities who seem to have it all but are never really happy. The only thing that will give purpose to your life is Jesus.

Celebrate the Children!

Some of Jesus' followers didn't think He had time to spend with children. They tried to get the kids to leave Him alone, but that's when He made this statement: "Let them come!"

Why did He say that God's kingdom belongs to people who are like children? Because children easily trust and don't argue about every point or need to have things proven to them. As people grow up they lose that trust sometimes.

Adults should be more like children. Childlike faith is much more pleasing to God because it is a faith that completely trusts Him.

> "Let the little children come to Me, and do not hinder them, for the kingdom of God belongs to such as these."
>
> Mark 10:14

Living It

Isn't it nice to hear something good about being a kid? Since you are young, you probably still have the kind of faith that just trusts God.

But, as life gets more complicated, that childlike faith gets harder to hold on to. You might start asking lots of questions and find that your trust in God slips once in a while. Try not to let that happen. Work now on making your faith as strong as possible so that your trust will remain childlike as you grow up.

Real Love

> "Love your enemies, do good to those who hate you, bless those who curse you, pray for those who mistreat you."
>
> Luke 6:27-28

You love your friends … big deal. It's easy to love people who love you back.

The real test of Christian love is whether you can love people who lie to you, bully you, say mean things or just generally treat you badly. Can you love them and pray for them even if they don't want your prayers and kindness?

That's the love Jesus wants you to be able to share.

Living It

Tess loves her friends and they love her. But one girl has a problem with Tess. Annie is really mean to her. She tells lies about her and tries to get Tess's friends mad at her.

When Tess says hi to her she says something mean about Tess's ugly clothes or messy hair. What does Tess do? She just loves Annie. She prays every day that Annie will have a good day and that she will know that Tess does truly love her. Tess's love = the love Jesus commanded.

February

Priceless Sparrows

> "Are not two sparrows sold for a penny? Yet not one of them will fall to the ground outside your Father's care."
>
> Matthew 10:29

Sparrows are common, ordinary birds. Sparrows are everywhere. They are really nothing special, except to God. He made them.

God knows what is happening with every bit of His creation. Even plain old sparrows matter to Him. Nothing happens to God's stuff without Him having a hand in it.

So a plain, unspectacular bird can't fall from the sky without God deciding on that action. That means He is in control of everything in your life! Cool? Yes!

Living It

Mandy doesn't feel special. She doesn't believe that she is very good at anything. She has a house full of brothers and sisters and because she is quiet she gets lost in the chaos. Mandy feels invisible. She even doubts that anyone really cares what happens to her.

At least, she used to feel that way – until she read this verse in Matthew. When she thinks about God paying that much attention to little birds, it's easier to believe that He really cares about her and has a plan for her life.

Brown-Sugar Verse

If you have ever made cookies with brown sugar as an ingredient, you know that you put brown sugar in the measuring cup, press it down and add more, press it down again and add more.

It's amazing how much sugar you can get in a measuring cup. Guess what? That's how God's blessings are to those who are generous. When you give, God gives, too. He just gives and gives and gives. You cannot imagine how much!

"Give, and it will be given to you. A good measure, pressed down, shaken together and running over, will be poured into your lap."
Luke 6:38

Living It

Marsha knows all about brown sugar because chocolate chip cookies are her specialty. Pressing brown sugar into the measuring cup is one of her favorite things to do (and then sneaking a mouthful or two). Marsha has also seen this Scripture verse in action in her grandmother's life. Gran is a generous person with her time, her energy and her money. It seems like the more Gran gives, the more she gets back in the form of friendships, help from people and just pure joy. It's proof for Marsha that you can never out-give God!

Let Your Light Shine!

"Let your light shine before others, that they may see your good deeds and glorify your Father in heaven."

Matthew 5:16

What light is Jesus talking about in this verse? Earlier in Matthew Jesus called Himself the Light of the world. So, it makes sense that when a girl accepts Jesus into her heart, His light shines inside her.

Jesus completed the light instruction with: **Let it shine!** When people know that you are a Christian and they see the light of your love and kind deeds shining then they give credit for it to God.

Your light is a witness to God!

Living It

Jane loves Jesus with all her heart. She also loves people. Jane is kind to everyone, even to people who aren't kind to her. Jane's love is not just convenient, it is also sacrificial.

She helps the older woman next door weed her garden. She studies with a friend who struggles with math. She does her chores without being asked. Jane loves and helps. People notice what she does and they praise God because they know Jane's love and service comes from Him.

Seed Taking Root

Just hearing God's Word is not enough. It's a good starting point, because you have to hear before you can believe, but it isn't enough.

What happens is that sometimes people hear the message of God's love, but they don't let it sink into their hearts. That gives Satan a chance to sneak in and steal that word away. Then their faith never takes root or grows.

"Some people are like seed along the path, where the Word is sown. As soon as they hear it, Satan comes and takes away the Word that was sown in them."

Mark 4:15

Living It

Jenna's parents have taken her to church since she was little. She has heard many times that God loves her and that Jesus died for her sins. But, she has never received Jesus as her Savior. Maybe she hopes that her parents' faith will get her into heaven.

Jenna is giving Satan a chance to steal away the Word of God and keep her away from Him. The best thing she can do is to ask Jesus into her heart so His Word can sink in and take root.

Harvest Workers

"The harvest is plentiful, but the workers are few. Ask the Lord of the harvest, therefore, to send out workers into His harvest field."

Luke 10:2

The world is full of people who do not yet know about the love of Jesus. Many people will accept Jesus if someone would just tell them about Him.

Jesus challenges all of His followers to do their part in sharing the message of His love with others in the world. Some people go around the world to tell of God's love. Some people give money to help those who go. Some people pray for the missionaries. Each one has a part in the harvest of those who come to Jesus.

Living It

Mallory's church is very supportive of missionary work. The church members believe that Jesus called people to go out to the world and share the message of His love.

Mallory's family prays for the missionaries that their church supports. Each member of the family saves money and gives it to the work of missions. Mallory knows that, even as a child, she is part of the work of harvesting the fields for Jesus.

Part of Jesus' Family

There is no room in Jesus' family for arguing or fighting. If the members of Jesus' family can't get along with each other, why would others want to be a part of it? That wouldn't be a good advertisement.

Jesus' followers should be bound together by their love for Him and their love for one another.

Don't let little things come between you and other Christians. Solve your differences quickly and let love be your guide.

> "By this all men will know that you are My disciples, if you love one another."
>
> John 13:35

Living It

Valerie and Missy are good friends. One thing they have in common is that they both love Jesus. They get along great and hardly ever argue, except for right now.

Missy hurt Val's feelings by something she said. Valerie could get mad and make a big deal about it, but she won't. She pays attention to Jesus' words and keeps peace with her friend. She talks to Missy and they resolve their differences. Their friends all know that they both love Jesus and now they only see love between the two friends.

Worship Only God

"Away from Me, Satan! For it is written: 'Worship the Lord your God, and serve Him only!'"

Matthew 4:10

Satan tried to get Jesus to worship him instead of God. After being tempted, Jesus told Satan to go away. Jesus said the Scriptures say to worship God and serve only Him.

There are two key things to notice here. One is that Jesus knew what was written in Scripture. That means we should know what is in Scripture, too. The second thing is that Jesus declared that God should be more important than anything else. Worship only God!

Living It

Caitlin says she does worship only God. But, if she's honest about what's important to her, she'll see that soccer is way more important than she realizes.

It's OK to love a sport and to work at getting good at it. But Caitlin practices for hours every day. When she isn't practicing soccer, she's thinking about it. She spends way more time thinking about and practicing soccer than she does thinking about God or reading His Word. Which do you think she worships more? Soccer or God?

Sharing the Wealth

Jesus was speaking to a rich young man who wanted to know what he had to do to be saved. Jesus told the man to give away all his wealth, but the rich man couldn't do that.

Now, there is nothing wrong with being rich. But sometimes money becomes more important to people than God, because wealthy people don't feel that they need God's help. They think their money can solve all their problems.

A person who has lots of money and generously shares with those who need help will certainly find it easy to enter the kingdom of God.

> "It is easier for a camel to go through the eye of a needle than for someone who is rich to enter the kingdom of God."
> Mark 10:25

Living It

By most people's standards, it appears that Sara and her family are rich. They have a beautiful home, expensive furniture and take exciting vacations. Sara has designer clothes and every techy gadget she could want.

They may be rich, but they take seriously what Jesus teaches about sharing what they have. They give a lot of money (and time) to helping others. They often invite people over to enjoy their beautiful home and share a meal. They share everything God has given them.

Fishing for People

> "Don't be afraid; from now on you will fish for people."
>
> Luke 5:10

Several of Jesus' first disciples were fishermen before they started following Him. That's how they earned their living.

When Jesus called His disciples to follow Him, He explained what their future held in ways they would understand. When Jesus said they would be fishing for people, He was saying they would now be winning people to faith in Him.

That would be their new career – fishing for souls!

Living It

Cori is not a fisherman. She has never even been fishing, but she knows that a fisherman puts bait on a hook and then puts it in the water to attract fish. So, she gets the concept that by sharing God's love with people, they have the chance to accept Jesus.

The mission of God's people is to share the story of His love with others. When others hear how much He loves them, they have the chance to accept Him as Savior. Cori understands that by sharing God's love she is "fishing for people" for Him!

Putting Love into Action

You can say that you love God. You can even think that you mean it. You certainly want to love Him. But, while saying you love Him and wanting to love Him is the first step, the real proof that you do love Him is when you obey Jesus' teachings.

They are all written down for you in the Bible so you can't say, "I would obey them, but I don't know them." If you say you love God, show it by reading His Word, learning His commands and obeying them.

"If you love Me, obey My commandments."
John 14:15

Living It

Mallory says she loves Jesus. She reads her Bible and prays every day. She is kind to others. When she hurts someone, she is quick to apologize. She is honest. She sacrifices for others by helping them when she would rather play and by cheering for a friend who receives an honor that Mallory wanted.

Andrea says she loves Jesus. She doesn't read her Bible, pray, help others, cheer for anyone. Andrea thinks she deserves the best of everything. Which girl obeys Jesus' commands?

Quiet Generosity

> "When you give to the needy, do not announce it with trumpets, as the hypocrites do in the synagogues and on the streets, to be honored by others. I tell you truly, they have received their reward in full."
>
> Matthew 6:2

Giving to the poor is a good thing to do. In fact, it's what Jesus said to do. However, bragging about your generosity so that others pat you on the back and compliment you does not please God.

A girl who gives to the needy just so others will notice and think, "Wow, she's so generous!" will not be rewarded by God. The pats on the back she receives are all the reward she will get!

Living It

Things have been pretty hard since Julie's dad lost his job. Sometimes there isn't even enough money for food. One morning a big box appeared on their front porch.

The box was filled with all kinds of food and even some small toys for Julie and her sister! There was no card or anything so Julie's family didn't even know who shared this generous gift, but God knew!

One Lost Sheep

Would you think that a man who had 100 sheep wouldn't even notice if one of them got lost? And, if he did, wouldn't it be more important to stay with the 99 sheep and keep them safe than to go look for the lost one?

Well, this is an illustration of how much God loves **you**! He would do anything to find you and bring you into His family. God's love is greater than anything!

"If a man owns a hundred sheep, and one of them wanders away, will he not leave the ninety-nine on the hills and go to look for the one that wandered off?"

Matthew 18:12

Living It

Sue has never felt special. It's hard to feel special when you have five brothers and sisters. Their house is always noisy and her mom and dad are always busy.

When Sue heard this story about the shepherd searching for one lost sheep she realized that she was like that sheep and God would search for her. She realized that Jesus loves *her* very much. That makes her feel very special!

The Kingdom of God

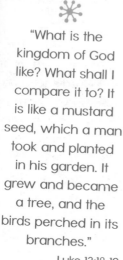

"What is the kingdom of God like? What shall I compare it to? It is like a mustard seed, which a man took and planted in his garden. It grew and became a tree, and the birds perched in its branches."

Luke 13:18-19

Jesus often compared God's kingdom to things that people understood. He did that so they would know how wonderful heaven is. A mustard seed is a tiny seed. God's kingdom starts small, too … in a single heart. But it grows and grows into many hearts.

By the time Jesus returns to take His children to heaven the kingdom will be bigger and more wonderful than you can imagine. It will be everything you can dream of.

Living It

Sam's friend, Ella, is not a Christian. Ella doesn't know that Jesus loves her. She doesn't know that He died for her and rose again. She doesn't know about God's kingdom.

Sam prays for Ella every day. She gently shares her faith with her friend. When Ella prays to accept Jesus into her heart, the kingdom of God grows bigger!

Leading Someone Astray

Jesus is very serious about sin. If a person leads another Christian into sin on purpose, she is in big trouble. The one who caused the sin is responsible for her own sin **and** the sin of the other person, too!

We all need to take seriously the command not to sin and to take care of one another so that we don't lead others into sin.

Pay attention!

> "If anyone causes one of these little ones – those who believe in Me – to stumble, it would be better for them if a large millstone were hung around their neck and they were thrown into the sea."
>
> Mark 9:42

Living It

"Come on, it's no big deal," Cynthia urged. But Annie wasn't so sure. "All you have to do is go in the store, pretend to be looking around, slide a candy bar into your pocket and then leave. It's fun! Come on, I dare ya!"

Annie knew what Cynthia suggested was wrong, but Cynthia was doing exactly what Jesus said not to do – leading someone else to sin. She will have to answer to God for this.

One Way

> "Whoever believes in Him is not condemned, but whoever does not believe stands condemned already because they have not believed in the name of God's one and only Son."
>
> John 3:18

There is one way to heaven and only one way. To be saved you must believe that Jesus is God's Son, His only Son, and that Jesus did not sin at all, but came to earth and died for your sins so that your heart could be clean.

God brought Jesus back to life and now He is alive, waiting to spend forever with you in heaven. If you don't believe this, you are not a member of God's family. Plain and simple.

Living It

Mary remembers the very moment that the truth of what Jesus did became clear in her mind. She knows the day when she understood that Jesus is God's Son and that He died for her sins.

Mary knows that she is saved and a member of God's family, because she believes in Jesus and has asked Him into her heart. That moment of decision changed her life forever!

Comfort When You Mourn

Mourning is more than just being sad. Mourning is when your heart aches because you are so sad.

Mourning happens when someone you love dies and you miss her very much. Jesus promises comfort for you when you are mourning.

The comfort comes from His love for you, His care for you and because He brings other loved ones into your life to help you. He does that because He loves you.

"Blessed are those who mourn, for they will be comforted."
Matthew 5:4

Living It

Jorie was so sad that her heart hurt. She was a little bit scared, too. Her mom died and Jorie missed her with all her heart. She wondered if anyone would care for her like her mom did.

Jorie prayed for help and sure enough God sent it! She knew He loved her and that was great, but she needed someone to hug her and tell her things would be OK, too. God sent Mom's sister, Aunt Maddie! They talked together, told stories about Mom, hugged each other and cried together. It made Jorie feel a lot better to have Aunt Maddie with her.

No-Show Prayers

"When you pray, do not be like the hypocrites, for they love to pray standing in the synagogues and on the street corners to be seen by others. Truly I tell you, they have received their reward in full."

Matthew 6:5

Jesus often instructed people to do things in private, not for a public show. Praying is an important part of our relationship with Jesus, but it is not meant to be a show.

Jesus said that to put on a big show of praying just so other people will think you are super spiritual actually makes you look like someone who is only pretending to know Him.

Prayer is between you and Jesus – even when you're praying in a group. Don't try to impress others with your prayers, just talk to Jesus.

Living It

Claire wants her friends to know that she loves Jesus because she really does. It's tempting to stand up in Sunday school and pray out loud long prayers with fancy words.

But, doing that just so others think Claire is super serious about Jesus would be wrong, as this verse says. Praying for show won't win you any super spiritual awards! Just pray from your heart.

Use It or Lose It

Did you know that every girl in God's family has a job? God gives you just what you need to do that job.

Each talent, skill and ability you have is a gift from Him and He wants you to use it to honor Him and share His love with others.

If a girl chooses not to use what God gives her or to use it for some purpose other than honoring Him, that talent and ability may be taken away!

"I tell you that to everyone who has, more will be given, but as for the one who has nothing, even what they have will be taken away."

Luke 19:26

Living It

Lisa sings like an angel. Seriously, she has a beautiful voice and people love to hear her sing. The cool thing is that Lisa loves to sing God's praises. She uses her gift to honor Him.

So, she actually gets more and more opportunities to sing for Him. He makes sure she gets lots of chances to sing. Many, many people are blessed by Lisa's gift, used for God!

The Best Food

"Do not work for food that spoils, but for food that endures to eternal life, which the Son of Man will give you. For on Him God the Father has placed His seal of approval."

John 6:27

Food is necessary for life. People work at jobs to earn money for food. A lot of time, energy and money are spent on food. Food is important.

But there is something even more important, and that is knowing and serving God. Jesus encouraged people to put their energy and focus on that kind of food.

Learn to know God by reading His Word and by serving and obeying Him. That will give you "food" that lasts forever.

Living It

Renee sees two types of people in her family. Both provide food for their families, but that isn't the issue. Uncle Joe puts all his energy into his career and getting more and more stuff. God isn't important to Him at all.

But Renee's parents are serious about God. They read their Bibles, pray with their kids and serve God. They provide food for their family now and they are laying up food in heaven. Renee wants to be just like her parents.

A Humble Example

Jesus doesn't ask His followers to live in a way that is impossible. We can be sure of that because His life is a model for the way we should live.

All we have to do is follow His example of humble service. Need proof? He made the statement in today's Scripture verse right after He washed His disciples' feet. That was a humble job to do for others – a job done by a servant. By doing it, Jesus showed His followers how to serve others humbly and quietly.

> "I have set you an example that you should do as I have done for you."
> John 13:15

 ## Living It

People say that Erica has a servant's heart. She doesn't even have to think about it. When someone needs something done and she knows she can help, Erica just gets busy and does it.

She is happy to help others by washing dishes, pulling weeds, babysitting. She will do anything and do it without bragging. She likes to serve others just as Jesus did. It makes her happy to help and she knows it makes Jesus happy, too.

The Holy Spirit

> "I will ask the Father, and He will give you another Advocate to help you and be with you forever – the Spirit of Truth."
>
> John 14:16-17

This is such an awesome promise from Jesus because the Advocate, the Spirit of Truth, is the Holy Spirit.

God sent Him to live in our hearts. Since He is in our hearts, He helps us know right from wrong and He is always with us. He guides us to know what is true and honest.

The Holy Spirit helps us serve God and reminds us how much He loves us, because He is always with us.

Living It

Danielle loves to read. She's always looking for a new book. When a friend loaned her a book, Danielle jumped right into it. But she had read only a few pages when she got a feeling that it might not be a good book for her.

The story had things in it that were not good to put into her mind. How did Danielle know that? The Holy Spirit in her heart nudged her to recognize that it wasn't stuff that would honor God. So, she gave the book back and found another one.

Giving Till it Hurts

Jesus compared a rich man who gave extra money to God's work to a widow who gave a couple of pennies. Maybe she didn't give much, but she gave all she had. She had nothing left. Jesus admired the widow because she held nothing back from God.

The rich man gave more actual money but it was only his extra money. The widow gave everything. Jesus looks at the heart of the giver and how much she holds back for herself compared with how much she is willing to give to others.

> "They all gave out of their wealth; but she, out of her poverty, put in everything – all she had to live on."
> Mark 12:44

Living It

Maddie was saving money to buy her own computer. She was getting pretty close to having enough. After her birthday, she finally had enough money for the laptop she wanted.

But then she heard about children in another country who didn't have clean water to drink. Maddie couldn't get the thought of them out of her mind. You know what Maddie did? She gave all of her computer money to the ministry that would send water to the children!

Rules of Love

> "I tell you that unless your righteousness surpasses that of the Pharisees and the teachers of the law, you will certainly not enter the kingdom of heaven."
>
> Matthew 5:20

The Pharisees and teachers of the law were the religious leaders of Jesus' day. They should have been the most righteous and the best ones at knowing and obeying Jesus' teachings. But they weren't.

Instead, they decided for themselves what was important and they obeyed those laws and made their own rules, too.

They didn't obey some of the most important laws of God – for example, loving others!

Living It

"Christianity is just a bunch of rules. I don't need that! I can make my own decisions," Laura announced to Paula. She knew Paula was a Christian, but Laura had been criticized by some Christians who insisted that everyone had to live by their rules.

There wasn't much room for love in their lives. Paula had to live her life of love in front of Laura for a long time before Laura saw the difference.

Finding Your Way

The easy way is not always the best way. Jesus noticed that many people choose the easy way through life – at least it appears to be the easy way.

It may seem that the wide open road is the best one, because it seems to have fewer rules and gives you more control over your own life.

However, the narrow way is the one that leads to God. This road takes you to love, care and protection. The door to the narrow way is opened by Jesus.

> "Enter through the narrow gate. For wide is the gate and broad is the road that leads to destruction, and many enter through it."
>
> Matthew 7:13

Living It

Lana never takes the easy way. She works hard at school. She does her chores well. She takes on challenges and is brave because she knows Jesus is with her.

So, when a friend challenges her choice to follow Jesus because it looks hard, Lana says, "No way!" She knows that the description of the narrow way doesn't mean harder, it means better, because it leads her to Jesus and the joy of knowing Him.

The Joy of Prayer

"Ask and it will be given to you; seek and you will find; knock and the door will be opened to you."

Matthew 7:7

What do you know about love? When you love someone you want to do things for that person. You want to help, care and give everything you can to that person.

Love is very giving. Well, guess what? Jesus loves you, too! He wants you to talk to Him. He wants to hear what you need and how you feel. You have the joy of praying. Tell Him what you need. Tell Him how you feel. Just talk with Jesus.

Living It

Ellen loves Jesus and she knows that He loves her. She is so thankful that she can talk with Jesus about whatever is on her heart.

Right now she is praying about a friend who is moving away. Ellen prays for her friend to make new friends and to like her school. Ellen asks God to take care of her friend and to help them stay in touch. She knows He will answer!

Source of Life

This statement shows that Jesus is the source of all life. Just as a vine brings food to its leaves and flowers, Jesus brings food to His children. He gives them the power and strength to grow and be healthy and strong.

Jesus is the connection to God, the Father of all things. Jesus said this to encourage His followers to stay close to Him so they could get the nutrition they need to grow.

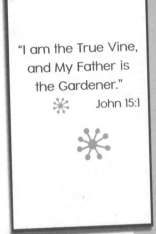

"I am the True Vine, and My Father is the Gardener."

John 15:1

Living It

Kara knows that eating healthy food helps her body grow strong. Junk food makes her body fat and doesn't give her energy. Good nutrition makes a strong body and a strong brain.

Kara has learned that Jesus does the same thing for her heart and spirit. She stays close to Him by reading her Bible which is His words to her. If she puts junk in her heart by what she listens to or reads, then her heart is kind of dirty. The closer Kara stays to Jesus, the healthier her heart is!

Party Time

> "In the same way, I tell you, there is rejoicing in the presence of the angels of God over one sinner who repents."
>
> Luke 15:10

Just in case you ever begin to feel that you do not matter to God, go back and read today's verse. Read it again and again.

Jesus made this statement after talking about how a woman looked everywhere to find one lost coin. When she found it all her friends came and celebrated with her!

Jesus loves **you** so much that when you repented of your sins and accepted Him as Savior, there was a paaarrrtttyyyy in heaven!

Living It

"Nothing special." That's how Stephanie used to describe herself. Average looks, average height, no special talents. Just plain old Stephanie.

However, when she thought about Jesus and the angels actually celebrating when she became a Christian, it made her smile. Yep, a real smile spread across her face and danced around in her heart. Then she began to feel pretty special!

Lip Service Only

Jesus is quoting from the book of Isaiah. Why is that important? Because it shows that Jesus knew the Scriptures.

If that was important for Jesus, it must certainly be important for us, too. Worshiping and honoring Jesus comes from the heart. You can say all the right words, but if your heart honors something or someone else, Jesus will know it. He sees your heart.

> "These people honor Me with their lips, but their hearts are far from Me."
>
> Mark 7:6

Living It

Linnie is not shy about much of anything. She quickly volunteers when her Sunday school teacher asks for someone to pray aloud. She offers her opinion in every discussion about God and the Christian life.

It seems that Linnie has all the answers, but God can see that none of those answers come from her heart. Linnie has not accepted Jesus as her Savior. So, her heart is far from God. She might be fooling the people around her, but she isn't fooling God.

Busy God

> "My Father is always at His work to this very day, and I, too, am working."
>
> John 5:17

God is never on vacation. He never takes a day off. God and Jesus are always paying attention to what is going on in the world and in your life.

This verse shows that God and Jesus are one – and that their work is the same. They both have the goal of bringing people into God's family and teaching, guiding and loving their family members.

You never have to worry about whether God knows what you're dealing with. He does.

Living It

Lizzie prayed that her grandpa would get well. He had been sick for a very long time. But he just kept getting sicker. Lizzie wondered if God was paying attention to her prayers. She wondered if He was busy with something else. She even wondered if He was on vacation or taking a day off.

But this verse promises her that God is always working. So she can trust Him to take care of things. She has to remember that God does things in His own time, not hers.

March

Hard to Love

> "If you love those who love you, what credit is that to you? Even sinners love those who love them."
>
> Luke 6:32

Do you love your friends and family? Of course you do! But Jesus said that isn't enough. He wants you to love people you don't know and even those who are mean to you.

The ability to do that is what sets you apart from people who don't know God. How do you do it? Let God love through you. He'll do the hard work, you just let Him.

Living It

Melanie gets along well with pretty much everyone. But one girl in her class just really annoys her. Kaylie brags about everything she does. She says unkind things about other kids. She's just not very nice.

Melanie knows that Jesus says she should love Kaylie, but she can't! However, she can ask God to love Kaylie through her. Then when unkind thoughts about Kaylie come into her mind, Melanie asks God to take them away and to love through her. Guess what? It works!

Good Fruit

When you go to an apple orchard, what kind of fruit do you expect to pick? Apples, right? Apple trees can't grow oranges or bananas. That's just silly.

Jesus is explaining that, just like trees are known to grow a certain fruit, people are known by how they live their lives. So, a person who claims to know Jesus will live a life that honors Him.

The "fruit" of a Jesus-follower's life will be love for Him and others and service to Him.

> "By their fruit you will recognize them. Do people pick grapes from thornbushes, or figs from thistles?"
>
> Matthew 7:16

Living It

"Liar! You are nothing but a liar!" Olivia hears those words a lot from friends because they are true. She lies about things she does or doesn't do. She lies about her friends. It's like she can't help herself. But, Olivia also says that she loves Jesus.

However, the fruit of her life doesn't match what should grow in the life of a Jesus-follower. Olivia must confess her sin, ask forgiveness and then get serious about her life, showing that she does love Jesus!

Evidence from Inside

> "What comes out of a person is what defiles them."
>
> Mark 7:20

What goes better with fresh-baked chocolate chip cookies than a glass of cold milk? But you open a fresh carton of milk, take a bite of the cookie and a gulp of milk … yuck! It's sour and tastes awful!

You see, the package looked really cool, but what came out of it told you that the product was no good.

Jesus said that a person can look really cool from the outside, but what comes out of her – her behavior, the way she treats others, her words – those things show that her heart is unclean if they do not honor God.

Living It

Betty has not asked Jesus into her heart. That's obvious from the way she treats her mom and dad. She is disobedient. She argues about almost everything, but especially about doing chores. Her words show little respect to her parents.

Betty's heart is evil, because Jesus hasn't made it clean. So what comes out of her mouth and her behavior shows how unclean she is inside. Betty needs Jesus.

A New Command

Jesus wants all of us who are His followers to love one another. If we can't get along, what makes us any different from those who do not know Jesus?

Jesus said to love one another as He loved us. What does that mean? He loved us so much that He died for us. That means we should love one another as much as possible – giving of our time, energy, priorities – whatever others need.

> "A new command I give you: Love one another. As I have loved you, so you must love one another."
>
> John 13:34

Living It

Who knew there would be cliques at church? Seriously, Rita and her family had just started coming to this new church.

Rita was having a hard time fitting in, even though she went to school with a couple of the girls. They didn't include her in any activities and she even heard one of them make an unkind remark about her. The girls at her new church were not showing love to Rita. They had not taken Jesus' command to heart to love one another.

Belief Instead of Fear

"Don't be afraid; just believe."

Mark 5:36

You can trust Jesus to take care of you. No matter what struggles life brings you, just believe in His power and strength.

Jesus spoke these words to a father who had just been told that his daughter was dead. Imagine hearing Jesus say not to be afraid, but to trust Him when someone you love very much has just died.

But the father did trust Jesus and his trust paid off. There is no situation Jesus can't handle – none.

Living It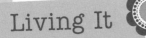

Sindra sits quietly at dinner. She tries very hard not to make a sound. She is careful not to draw attention to herself. Her dad has been drinking again and he gets really mean when he drinks.

She is afraid that he will hurt her or her mom if she does anything to make him angry. She wants to believe that Jesus will take care of her and her mom and protect them from her dad. Believing is hard, but she is learning more each day how to do it.

Jesus Meets Your Needs

Some people reach out to Jesus just for the miracles they think He will do for them. They view Jesus as some giant Santa Claus in the sky.

Their relationship with Jesus is one-sided and based fully on what He can do for them. Others reach out to Jesus because they see that He meets their every need.

He loves them and takes care of them.

> "Very truly I tell you, you are looking for Me, not because you saw the signs I performed but because you ate the loaves and had your fill."
>
> John 6:26

Living It

Lisa wanted to get an A on the big history exam. She wanted it badly, but not enough to study hard. She decided to pray that God would help her get an A.

Then she went out and played with her friends, played video games, and read a book. She did everything except study. She thought Jesus would do a miracle for her. Instead, Lisa failed the test and found out that God would not do miracles for her when she didn't do her part.

Resting in Jesus

"Come to Me, all you who are weary and burdened, and I will give you rest."

Matthew 11:28

Jesus knows that life for us will not always be easy. He didn't promise to make it easy by taking away our problems. He did promise to go through the hard times with us.

We can lean on Him, which is sort of like leaning against a wall or a chair when you are really tired. He will help us rest and give us the needed strength to keep on going.

The best way to get relief from stress and tiredness is to stay close to Jesus.

Living It

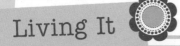

Homework. Gymnastic team classes every day. Piano practice. Chores at home. Family times. Even a kid has a lot to do every day. Add to that stress, like parents who don't always get along, friends who get mad at you, little brother issues ... and yeah, life gets stressful.

How do you get through these tough times? Come close to Jesus. Close the door of your room, be alone with Him, tell Him what is wearing you out and just let Him love you.

Remember!

Jesus gave this instruction to His disciples at the Last Supper – the meal they shared before He was arrested.

He told them that when they ate the bread and drank the wine they should remember Him. He didn't mean they should just remember their friend named Jesus. They should remember what He did for them (and us) by His death and re-surrection.

He gave the ultimate gift of love.

"This is My body given for you; do this in remembrance of Me."
Luke 22:19

Living It

Every time Terra eats Mike and Ike® candy, she thinks of her friend Sam who moved away a while ago. They both loved those chewy candies and often shared a box. Terra thinks it is cool that the candy reminds her of her friend. It's nice to have a connecting point. That's what the communion service at church is, too. When Terra takes the bread and the grape juice, she remembers Jesus and His gift of dying for her sin and coming back to life. It is a reminder that she will be with Him in heaven someday. It's a connecting time of thankfulness for her.

Whole-Hearted Service

"No one can serve two masters. Either you will hate the one and love the other, or you will be devoted to the one and despise the other. You cannot serve both God and money."

Matthew 6:24

Following God half-heartedly is not following God at all. If He doesn't have all the devotion of your heart, then whatever is claiming the other part of it will eventually push God out of the way.

For a lot of people money becomes their passion – getting more and more of it. There's nothing wrong with money unless you think more about getting money than you do about God.

Living It

Katie notices what people do. For example, she sees her parents put God first in everything. They give generously when there is any special need around the world and even when there isn't. Their money is God's, not theirs.

She sees others who say they love God, but who spend a lot of time working to make more and more money. They give some away but not much. Sure, they have really nice stuff, but do they love and serve God? Doesn't look like it.

Just Believe

Jesus spoke these words to a father who asked Jesus to help his son who was demon-possessed.

Jesus made it sound so simple – just believe and anything is possible. It isn't simple, but it is true. The father asked Jesus to help him believe more. He knew his faith wasn't strong enough, but that Jesus could help it grow!

> "Everything is possible for one who believes."
> Mark 9:23

Living It

Brittany wants to believe what this Scripture verse says. She wants to so much, because her mom is sick, very sick. Brittany has asked God to heal her mom. It hasn't happened yet, but Brittany knows that He could heal her, if it is His will. She knows that sometimes God doesn't do the things we ask, but she keeps praying because she believes He loves her and her mom.

She asks God to help her believe more and more. The good thing is that Brittany knows that Jesus loves her mom even more than she does. She believes He will do what is best for her.

Do Likewise

"Go and do
likewise."

Luke 10:37

Jesus often taught His followers by telling stories. After all, who doesn't enjoy a good story?

On this particular day, He had just told the story of the Good Samaritan. Perhaps you know the story: a man is beaten up by robbers. Two different men pass by the poor victim – church men – but they don't help. A third man passes him, a man from Samaria, sworn enemies of the Jews. But this Samaritan stops to help.

Jesus finished the story by asking which of the three men was a neighbor to the hurt man. When they answered the third man, Jesus said, "Be like him!"

Living It

Carol has a mentor. Well, she wouldn't call her friend a mentor, but that's what she is. Carol's friend is always kind and helpful to everyone she meets and even to those who aren't very nice.

Carol watches her friend be kind and helpful to people who don't return that kindness and she decides, "I want to be like her." That's exactly what Jesus suggested – follow a leader who is following Jesus.

God's Care

Jesus knows everything about you. He knows everything that happens to you. Absolutely nothing surprises Him.

Look around you and see the birds flying around. They have food and water. God takes care of them. You matter much more to Him than those birds. He even knows how many hairs there are on your head!

Every detail is known to Him and He cares about them all!

> "Even the very hairs of your head are all numbered. So don't be afraid; you are worth more than many sparrows."
>
> Matthew 10:30-31

Living It

Some days Jana and her mom don't have enough food to eat. Her mom lost her job and hasn't been able to pay the rent for a while. They are in danger of losing their home. Life looks pretty scary.

Jana tries to pray, but she feels like God isn't paying attention to their problems. He is, though. Deep down inside, she knows He is and she trusts Him to take care of them whatever happens. Jana trusts that she and her mom matter to God.

Shallow-Root Christians

> "Others, like seed sown on rocky places, hear the Word and at once receive it with joy. But since they have no root, they last only a short time. When trouble or persecution comes because of the Word, they quickly fall away."
>
> Mark 4:16-17

Jesus explained how some people receive the news of God's love by comparing it with how seeds take root in certain kinds of soil.

Some people hear the news of God's love and get excited about it. But they don't read their Bibles and pray in order to learn to trust God and grow stronger faith.

When problems come, they don't have enough faith to keep trusting God.

Living It

Stella loves singing praise choruses. She recently learned about God's love for her so singing gives her goose bumps and makes her feel happy. But she doesn't read her Bible or pray very often.

So, when one of her old friends gives her a hard time about believing in God, she quickly turns away from Him and goes back to hanging out with her non-Christian friends. The roots of her faith are too shallow to keep her strong.

Doing Good

Helping only people who help you is not obeying Jesus. Being nice to only those who are nice to you is not obeying Jesus. Anyone can do that, even if she doesn't know Jesus at all.

Real evidence that a person's heart wants to serve Jesus is when she serves God and loves Him. But this doesn't happen without God's help.

Loving **all** people, not just your friends is the goal Jesus has for you!

> "If you do good to those who are good to you, what credit is that to you? Even sinners do that."
>
> Luke 6:33

Living It

You help your friend with her math homework because you're good at it and she isn't. Or, maybe you do your sister's chores because she is busy. You're helping your friends or loved ones.

But what if a girl who is usually mean to you needs to have her homework delivered when she is sick at home? Would you do it? If you obey Jesus, you will. Anyone can be kind to those who are friendly to her. Being nice to your enemies is done because Jesus' love is flowing through you!

Knowing Jesus

> "Everyone who drinks this water will be thirsty again, but whoever drinks the water I give them will never thirst. Indeed, the water I give them will become in them a spring of water welling up to eternal life."
>
> John 4:13-14

Everyone looks for something that makes them feel satisfied and complete. Some people want to be super popular. Some work to be the best student in their class. Some dream of being a famous singer or athlete or writer.

Whatever it is, these people look for satisfaction everywhere, except from Jesus. He says that their happiness will never last if they don't get their satisfaction from knowing and loving Him. That's what lasts forever.

Living It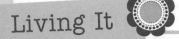

The popular girls are the coolest. They hang out together and giggle and hardly talk to anyone else. Paula wants more than anything to be one of them. She believes that it would truly make her happy.

Paula doesn't know that she would be working all the time to stay in the group and find her place. The only thing that will really make Paula happy is to accept Jesus and put all her energy into serving Him.

By the Book

Jesus said the words of today's Scripture verse to John the Baptist. He had just asked John to baptize Him and John tried to stop Him. Instead, John said that **he** should be baptized by Jesus.

But Jesus always paid attention to what was right. He didn't want anyone to be able to say that He wasn't truly the Messiah because things didn't happen the way the prophets said they would.

He wanted to do things by the book. If Jesus lived by the Book (the Bible), then so should we.

"Let it be so now; it is proper for us to do this to fulfill all righteousness."
Matthew 3:15

Living It

Lisa knew all the right things to say. She could pray out loud using fancy words. But she had never actually asked Jesus to be her Savior.

She was banking on the fact that her parents were Christians so she thought she could make it into heaven by going with them. Lisa had to learn that there are no shortcuts to serving God. She had to accept Jesus herself and do things "by the Book," just like Jesus did!

Jesus Is the Strongest!

> "I have told you these things, so that in Me you may have peace. In this world you will have trouble. But take heart! I have overcome the world."
>
> John 16:33

This world is full of all kinds of troubles. Jesus was speaking to His disciples when He said these words.

Jesus knew that even people who follow Him would have trouble. Sometimes the troubles come just because we follow Him. The world doesn't get why we follow and obey Jesus. He promised to give peace to those who follow Him. He promised that He would be with us.

And, He reminds us that no matter what kind of troubles the world throws at us … He will win!

Living It

Kathy recently asked Jesus into her heart. None of her friends are Christians so this is a new thing for her. Kathy knows that becoming a Christian does not mean she will stop having problems.

But her old friends get really angry about her new faith. She is thankful for this verse that reminds her that Jesus is stronger than anyone who is against her. She will get through difficult times by staying close to Him!

Jesus Sees the Truth

The day will come when every person will stand before God. Each person will have to answer for her choice of whether or not to accept Jesus as Savior.

People who have spent their lives only pretending to be Christians when it was convenient, will find out that they cannot fool God. He will separate the believers from the unbelievers.

He looks at people's hearts and sees the truth.

"All the nations will be gathered before Him, and He will separate the people one from another as a shepherd separates the sheep from the goats."
Matthew 25:32

Living It

Charlotte is a great actress. She can fool everyone into thinking she has real faith in Jesus. Yep, she knows all the right things to say. She even does good things like helping others, but Jesus isn't her motivation.

Yes, Charlotte can fool lots of people, but she can't fool God. He sees her heart and He knows she has not asked Jesus to be her Savior. She can't be a part of His family by pretending.

Be Careful What You Think

"Why do you entertain evil thoughts in your hearts?"

Matthew 9:4

Entertaining things in your heart is a choice. It means letting your mind and heart think about doing things that are not the way God wants you to think.

Jesus knew that sometimes people choose to think evil thoughts that pull them away from God. Evil thoughts can lead to questioning God about many things.

The Bible tells us to guard our hearts because Satan gets into our lives through hearts that aren't guarded. Keep your heart focused on God, His love for you and the truths of the Bible. Then there is no room for evil thoughts.

Living It

It's OK to ask questions, because you will never understand everything about God or about the Christian life.

But, entertaining evil thoughts is like what Callie did when she started accusing God of not loving her and not taking care of her. When Callie had those kinds of thoughts her heart focused on evil things, not on God's love and care.

Mercy Is as Mercy Does

God treats each of His children with mercy. He is kind and forgiving toward them. Jesus told us to treat others that way, too.

We receive kindness and forgiveness from God, even when we do not deserve it. Since we have been treated so kindly, we should treat others in the same way.

Our Father (isn't it cool to know that God is our Father?) wants us to do so.

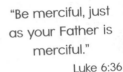

"Be merciful, just as your Father is merciful."

Luke 6:36

Living It

Emily is nice to pretty much everyone. The person she has the most trouble with is her little brother, Sam. He is such a pain! When Sam went into her room and destroyed it, Emily was ready to pound him!

Then she remembered how God is always merciful and forgiving to her. Over and over she needs and receives His mercy. Emily forgave Sam and even offered to play a game with him that night. She received mercy so she gave mercy.

Serving by Caring

"Take care of My sheep."

John 21:16

Peter was a close friend to Jesus. He was one of Jesus' disciples. One time, after Peter had told people he didn't even know Jesus, the two of them were talking.

Jesus wanted to know how Peter really felt about Him so He asked Peter three times if he really loved Jesus. Of course Peter answered yes each time. After each answer, Jesus gave him something to do – this time it was "feed My sheep."

Loving Jesus is more than just saying words. When you love Him, you serve Him, and that means action.

Living It

Sara is 10 years old. She wondered what she could do to take care of others. Sara took this instruction from Jesus seriously so she sat down with her friend, Suzie, and they came up with the "2S" Servant Plan.

The "2S" girls visit elderly neighbors, volunteer to babysit (for free) for busy moms, serve in the nursery at church, and pretty much any other way they can think of to help others and serve God. Can you think of some ways, too?

For or Against

Maybe you've heard the old saying, "Not to decide is to decide." That's what Jesus is saying here.

Once a person has heard about Jesus' love, then it is her responsibility to choose to accept Jesus or not. Saying, "Oh, I'll decide later" is really deciding not to accept Him.

So, if you aren't for Jesus then you are against Him – not a good place to be.

> "Whoever is not with Me is against Me, and whoever does not gather with Me scatters."
> Matthew 12:30

Living It

What does it look like to be against Jesus? Well, a person who is against Him would pull others away from Him. She would encourage others not to believe in Him or trust His Word. She would not be loving, kind and merciful to others. She would be the opposite of everything Jesus is.

On the other hand, being "with Jesus" means that He lives in her heart and guides her footsteps, her thoughts and her actions in ways that honor Him and pull others closer to Him.

Family Ties

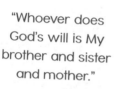

> "Whoever does God's will is My brother and sister and mother."
>
> Mark 3:35

Family relationships are the closest relationships on earth. Family members can be themselves with each other. They love each other totally (even if they don't always like each other).

Being a member of God's family is an unbelievable honor. It's only possible because Jesus, God's Son, came to earth, lived and died for our sins and then rose again to life. He said that anyone can be a member of His family by doing God's will, which means obeying Him and loving Him.

Living It

Erica has a cool family. She loves her parents, sister and brother, even if her little brother does sometimes make her crazy. She has good friends, too, but no one on earth is more important to her than her family. That helps her understand the privilege of being a member of God's family. It's the closest relationship.

Erica understands "doing God's will" to mean that she obeys Him, which means reading His Word so she knows what to obey. It means serving Him by loving Him and loving others. Doing God's will is living a life of love.

"Prove it" Prayers

In the middle of Satan tempting Jesus to turn away from God, Jesus quoted this Scripture verse from the Old Testament to him.

This is important because it proved that Jesus knew the Scriptures and if it was important enough for Him to know, then we should know it, too.

It's also important because it says that we shouldn't test God's love for us by saying, "If You love me You will do … such and such."

God **does** love us and He does what is best for us. He proves it every day.

> "It is said: 'Do not put the Lord your God to the test.'"
> Luke 4:12

Living It

"OK, God, if You really do love me like You say You do, then let me get Mrs. Ellingsen for English next year. If I get her then I'll know that You love me," Tiffany prayed.

Yeah, putting God to the test is not such a good idea. He doesn't answer your prayers just to prove something. He does what is best for you and shows you every day that He loves you. Don't do "prove it" kinds of prayers. Just trust Him.

Loving Service

> "Now that I, your Lord and Teacher, have washed your feet, you also should wash one another's feet."
>
> John 13:14

Imagine having your feet washed by the Son of God. It would be pretty humbling, wouldn't it?

Jesus did wash His disciples' feet even though that is a job usually done by servants. His act was a beautiful example of a servant's heart that serves others in basic, simple and unglamorous ways. It serves out of love.

Jesus told His disciples (and us) that we should do the same.

Living It

When the church van pulled into the parking lot after a long, hot day at the amusement park all the kids piled out. The youth pastor and other adults looked tiredly at the candy wrappers, water bottles and other stuff left in the van.

Then they heard a small voice say, "I'll clean it up while you make sure all the parents are here." Terra, one of the youngest girls, volunteered to serve them and the entire group by cleaning out the van. She served them, just as Jesus served His disciples by washing their feet. Love in action!

The Power of Prayer

Jesus wanted His followers to believe in Him and understand His amazing power. He wanted them to trust Him completely.

> "If you believe, you will receive whatever you ask for in prayer."
> Matthew 21:22

This statement sounds a little unbelievable – like you could get whatever you want from God. That makes Him sound like a big Santa Claus, doesn't it? But it isn't that simple.

When you believe in Jesus, read the Bible and try to obey God, then you end up wanting what He wants for you and accepting His answers to your prayers as what is best for you.

Living It

Abby read this verse in Matthew. "Hmm," she wondered, "so if I believe in God then I can ask for anything and I'll get it? Like, um, to be the most popular girl in school?"

Abby doesn't quite get it, does she? If she spends time reading God's Word and learning to serve Him, then the "wants" she prays for will slowly be turned to things that God actually wants to give her! Her desires will begin to match His!

Stay Focused

> Jesus replied, "No one who puts a hand to the plow and looks back is fit for service in the kingdom of God."
>
> Luke 9:62

There is important work for each of Jesus' followers to do. He knows that sometimes your job requires a lot of focus and concentration. It isn't possible to do the work well if you are looking around at other people and other things.

Just as a farmer has to watch where he's going if he is going to plow a straight line, God's worker needs to pay attention to what she is doing and where she is going.

Living It

"McKenna, please fold the laundry for me," Mom said. But McKenna didn't want to do that job. She wanted to unload the dishwasher. She folded one towel, then wandered into the kitchen to watch her sister put the dishes away.

McKenna didn't stay focused on her job. That's what Jesus is talking about in today's verse – looking around at other things instead of paying attention to your own job. This is especially important when doing a job God gives you to do. Pay attention and do it well!

Follow the Leader

Several of the men Jesus called to be His disciples were fishermen before meeting Him. When He asked each of them to follow Him, He wanted them to know what their new jobs would be – fishing for people.

Kind of a weird thing to say, eh? But Jesus was calling them to the job of telling people about God's love, encouraging people to believe that Jesus is the Son of God. Pretty cool job!

"Come, follow Me," Jesus said, "and I will send you out to fish for people."
Mark 1:17

Living It

Sophia wanted more than **anything** to be popular. She watched this one group of girls every day at school. She tried to copy their style of clothes. She wanted to do what they did and like what they liked. But Sophia didn't pay attention to what kind of people she was following. She didn't see how mean they were to other girls and how self-centered they were.

Be careful who you follow. You don't know where they will lead you. Jesus laid it out for His followers. They knew that if they followed Him they would be winning people for God.

Action, Not Show

> Jesus answered, "It is written: 'Man shall not live on bread alone, but on every word that comes from the mouth of God.'"
>
> Matthew 4:4

During Jesus' time on earth, some people fasted (went without food) for a few days at a time just to show how spiritual they were.

They weren't really that connected to God. They were actually just trying to show off. Jesus blew their cover by saying that fasting or eating was not the important thing – knowing and obeying God's Word is what really matters.

Show-offs are just show-offs. Loving God comes from the heart.

Living It

Heather brags about all the good stuff she does. She wants to make sure that everyone knows when she helps another person. She quotes Bible verses and sings popular choruses.

Heather thinks all this stuff proves that she really loves God. But Heather doesn't understand the Bible verses and she doesn't really, truly care about others. She is all show and no real action. Loving God comes from the heart. Bragging means nothing. Knowing God's Word and obeying Him is what really matters.

Born Again

A man asked Jesus some questions about who Jesus was and why He was able to do such amazing miracles. Jesus had a simple answer as to what would help this man understand His work. He said, "You must be born again."

Being born again is not a physical kind of birth, it's a birth of the heart. You are born again when you ask Jesus to come into your heart. He does this through the power of the Holy Spirit and then you are born into His family. Then, all that God does and the words of the Bible make sense to you.

> "You should not be surprised at My saying, 'You must be born again.'"
>
> John 3:7

Living It

Erica goes to Sunday school and church every week. But not because she really "gets" the whole God thing. She goes because she has friends there and usually there are fun things going on.

But, when the teacher starts the lesson or the minister begins His sermon, Erica tunes out. None of it makes any sense to her. It won't until the day she asks Jesus to forgive her sins and be her Savior – when she is born again.

A New Viewpoint

> "Open your eyes and look at the fields! They are ripe for harvest."
>
> John 4:35

Jesus' disciples didn't always understand why He took the time to stop and talk with certain people.

The harvest He mentions is not crops, it is people. He wanted all people to know God. That was His harvest.

The disciples needed to stop looking at things from a human viewpoint such as, "Why does Jesus take time to talk with people who are losers?" Their eyes needed to be opened to God's viewpoint, that all people need to know God!

Living It

When Jamie read these words of Jesus she prayed that He would open her eyes. He did ... to Patti. Patti didn't have cool clothes. Her hair wasn't styled in an attractive way. She wasn't good at sports or music and not especially smart. Most kids made fun of her – even to her face. "What a loser."

The thing is, none of them took the time to get to know her. God helped Jamie see Patti as a person – one who needed to know God's love. So, Jamie and Patti became friends and then Jamie could share God's love with her friend.

April

Good Hunger

> "Blessed are those who hunger and thirst for righteousness, for they will be filled."
>
> Matthew 5:6

Everyone hungers for something. Some people want fame or power. Some want lots of money. Some want success. Some just want to win at whatever they are doing and they are quick to criticize anyone who isn't a winner by their standards. Most people hunger for things they don't have.

Jesus' words here are a challenge to hunger and thirst for God – for the purpose of pleasing and serving Him, and seeing His will be done in your life. If that's what you want, you will have your desires granted.

Living It

God planted a real desire to know and serve Him in Emily's heart. Some of her friends were constantly striving for things like being first chair in the band, achieving the best time in cross country, and being popular.

There is nothing wrong with these things, but Emily's focus was for everyone to be treated fairly and for all people to have food and water. More than anything, she longed for all the people of earth to have the opportunity to know God's love. Yes, she hungered for that!

Us Against Them

"I tell you, love your
enemies and pray
for those who
persecute you,
that you may be
children of your
Father in heaven.
He causes His sun
to rise on the evil
and the good, and
sends rain on the
righteous and the
unrighteous."
Matthew 5:44-45

In Jesus' day an attitude developed of "us against them." Unfortunately that attitude is still around. People are divided by what they believe or by what they like.

Girls hang around with people just like them and are snarky toward anyone who is different. Jesus' response to this behavior was, "Stop it." You should love your enemies as much as you love your friends. God does, and blesses all people, not just the ones who agree with Him.

Living It

Maria and Stella ran against each other for class president. They each had their supporters and the campaign got ugly. There was name-calling and nasty tricks. By election day, Maria and Stella were flat-out enemies.

Stella won the election and Maria and her friends were angry. But then Maria remembered what Jesus taught. She texted congrats to Stella and promised to help and support her in any way she could.

Grow Up!

> "Be perfect, therefore, as your heavenly Father is perfect."
>
> Matthew 5:48

Perfect? Was Jesus kidding? No one is perfect except Him, right? Well, the Greek word Jesus used for perfection means something like maturity. So, actually Jesus was saying, "Grow up. Act your age."

He said this in the middle of the Sermon on the Mount, which gives a lot of instruction on how to live for God and how to treat others.

So, He's saying, "Put what I've taught you to practice in your life. Live maturely."

Living It

"Get out of my room! You're such a brat!" Kerri screamed at her brother. He looked scared as he ran down the hall. Kerri slammed her bedroom door and threw herself on the bed. She knew what was coming. The door opened and Mom said, "Kerri, you're five years older than Ryan. I know brothers can be a pain sometimes. But, you should behave more maturely.

You're a Christian so you know what Jesus taught about loving others. Do you think you just did that?" Kerri gulped. "No. I'll apologize to Ryan. I'm sorry, Mom."

All about God

People have often wondered why bad things happen to good people. Some think the bad things that happen are punishment for sin.

That's what the men talking to Jesus suggested about a man who was born blind. They thought that his blindness was punishment for his parents' sin. But Jesus turned their thoughts to another direction. Sometimes bad things just happen.

What's important is that God is glorified – either by taking away the bad thing or by the person's trust in Him during the hard times. It's all about God, not people.

> "Neither this man nor his parents sinned," said Jesus, "but this happened so that the works of God might be displayed in him."
>
> John 9:3

Living It

Mandy's aunt has cancer and Mandy is afraid she will die. She prays for her aunt all the time. "God, Aunt Sue loves You. She's helpful and caring to others and lots of people love her. Why does this have to happen to her? Won't You heal her?"

Mandy hasn't noticed how strong Aunt Sue's trust in God is. She knows He loves her and will take care of her, no matter what. He is glorified by her trust during this illness.

All the Way In!

> "Whoever wants to be My disciple must deny themselves and take up their cross daily and follow Me."
>
> Luke 9:23

This is Jesus' no-holds-barred definition of what it means to follow Him. You've got to be all the way in or you're not in at all.

Being a follower of Jesus means life is all about Him – loving Him, obeying Him, living for Him, learning more about Him. A true disciple cannot hold back a part of her life – such as where she goes on the Internet, or how she treats other kids.

Life is **all** about following Jesus.

Living It

Nora has a secret. No one knows about it, because it's in her thoughts. She likes to let her mind wander to think about things that she knows would not make Jesus proud.

Nora thinks that if no one knows about her thoughts then it can't color their opinion of her Christianity. But, Jesus knows. He knows that she isn't all the way in to following Him, because she is holding this area of her thoughts back. Following Jesus means getting all the way in!

True Rest

Jesus knows that life is stressful sometimes. You can be buried under a load of schoolwork. Family problems can be so constant. Tensions in your friendships are exhausting.

Yeah, there is a lot for you to deal with every day. Jesus knew that and He offered a solution – Himself.

His strength and gentleness will get you through whatever problems you face. Rest in Him.

"Take My yoke upon you and learn from Me, for I am gentle and humble in heart, and you will find rest for your souls."

Matthew 11:29

Living It

Myra hid her head under her pillow. Her parents were fighting again. "I can't take this anymore. I want to run away. Make them stop!" she prayed.

The fights happened night after night and sometimes it got pretty scary. As Myra lay in the darkness, she prayed once more, "Help me, Jesus. Help me." A warmth of peace floated over her like a soft blanket. Jesus answered that prayer and Myra found rest in Him.

Forgiven Much

"Therefore, I tell you, her many sins have been forgiven – as her great love has shown. But whoever has been forgiven little loves little."

Luke 7:47

These words were spoken to a religious leader – a man who thought he lived a pretty righteous life. He didn't think he had sinned much so he didn't think he really needed forgiveness from Jesus.

But, Jesus pointed out a woman who had lived a sinful life. She knew that she had been forgiven for a lot so she worshiped Him more fully.

Understanding how much Jesus has done for you makes you love Him even more!

Living It

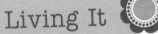

Kristin thinks she is just about perfect. She thinks she has life all figured out and that everything she does is right on. She has accepted Jesus, but doesn't really think about Him much because she doesn't really see why she needs to.

Sara has allowed Jesus to soften her heart and make her aware of the times she falls short in living for Him. She asks His forgiveness often and knows that He gives it. Sara loves Jesus with all her heart and is thankful for His grace and forgiveness.

Which girl has it right?

Great Eyesight!

The Pharisees – religious leaders of Jesus' time – thought they knew everything. But they didn't. They were living by rules they made up, not God's commands, and insisting that everyone follow their rules.

They were the blind leading the blind. Jesus warned His followers about following the Pharisees' rules and thinking they were obeying God by doing so. They weren't.

"If the blind lead the blind, both will fall into a pit."
Matthew 15:14

Living It

Kendra wanted to be in the popular crowd so badly she could taste it, and she had a chance. Caroline, the leader of the crowd, had suddenly taken an interest in Kendra for some reason.

She told Kendra ways to style her hair and what kind of clothes to wear. But one time when Caroline saw Kendra talking to a girl she had been friends with for years but who wasn't popular – and never would be – she told Kendra to dump that friend. Kendra's eyes were opened then. If she followed everything Caroline said that would be like the blind leading the blind.

Be Careful What You Say

> "The things that come out of a person's mouth come from the heart, and these defile them."
>
> Matthew 15:18

Words have so much power! Can you recall a time when someone said something hurtful to you? It took a long time to get over it, didn't it? (If you have yet.)

Jesus said the words that fly out of our mouths show what kind of stuff is going on in our hearts. If you're selfish, mean-spirited and prideful then all that stuff will show by the words you speak to others.

Clean up your heart and your words will clean up, too.

Living It

Vera puts on a good show of how nice she is. But Cathy knows it's all a show. She catches the brunt of Vera's unkind words and hurtful comments. It's almost like hatred is flying at Cathy from Vera.

All the effort she makes to seem kind and caring is lost. Her true heart is revealed by how she speaks to others. Vera has an unkind, selfish heart. She needs Jesus to clean it up for her.

A Personal Choice

Peter was one of Jesus' closest friends. Sometimes Peter spouted words before he thought, but there was no doubt that he loved Jesus.

In this conversation, Jesus asks Peter if people are saying that He truly is God's Son. After Peter answered that question Jesus asked this one: "What about you, Peter? Who do you say I am?"

You see, faith in Jesus is a personal decision. You don't become a Christian just because your parents are or just because you hang out with church kids. It's your choice – accept Jesus personally.

> "But what about you?" Jesus asked. "Who do you say I am?"
> Matthew 16:15

Living It

Faith's parents are Christians and their Christianity means a lot to them. They have family devotions every day. They love God and serve Him enthusiastically. They even named their girls, Faith, Hope and Grace.

Since Faith has grown up with Christianity being a part of every day, she just assumes she's a Christian, too. But it doesn't work that way. Faith needs to confess that Jesus is God's Son who died for her sins and rose again. She must ask Him personally to be her Savior.

Jesus Freak!

"If the world hates you, keep in mind that it hated Me first."

John 15:18

Jesus wasn't popular with some people. The ones who hated Him the most were actually the religious leaders. Weird, eh? They didn't like that He taught different things than they did. They didn't like that He didn't keep all the rules they had made up.

Since they hated Jesus, it only made sense that they hated His followers, too. That still happens sometimes today. People who are against God will be against His followers. That's OK, just keep on doing what God wants you to do. He will take care of them.

Living It

Betty got a part in the school play! She was so excited. But as she got into the part she found out that her character was supposed to use God's name in a way that made her uncomfortable.

Betty went to the director and asked if she could change the word and the director made fun of her in front of the whole cast. She called Betty a Jesus freak. That's OK. Betty knows she did the right thing so she treats the director with respect, but holds her ground on changing the words in the script.

Too Proud to Love

Jesus never had any good to say about people who draw attention to themselves. Some people think so highly of themselves that they feel they are above other people and entitled to be treated better. They like to get what they want and be first all the time.

There is absolutely nothing in this behavior that shows love, and God is all about love. Jesus will take care of those people because they will have to answer to Him for their inflated view of themselves.

> "All those who exalt themselves will be humbled, and those who humble themselves will be exalted."
> Luke 18:14

Living It

Linnie is a friendly girl. She talks to everyone. She is kind to everyone. She's just a nice girl. So it's hard for her to understand why Dawn behaves so unkindly toward her. Sure, Dawn is popular and she's smart and her parents have a lot of money.

But Dawn is so impressed with herself that she thinks she's too important to even say hello to Linnie or anyone else whom she doesn't think is important. Not very nice. Dawn is not showing love to others. She's too filled with pride to show love. That's not how Jesus teaches people to live.

Revealing Light

"Everyone who does evil hates the light, and will not come into the light for fear that their deeds will be exposed."

John 3:20

What specific light is Jesus referring to in this statement? Himself! Earlier this month He said, "I am the Light of the world."

Now He is just pointing out that people who enjoy doing wicked things will stay away from Him because otherwise they have to face their own sinfulness. It's easier to deny that you are a sinner if you think no one knows what you do.

But, when you stand near Jesus (the Light), everything is revealed.

Living It

Bullies are classic examples of staying away from the light. They get away with pushing other kids around and saying rotten things as long as no one stands up to them.

But, when a bully is confronted with the truth and passion of Jesus' love, all their ugliness is revealed to their own hearts, and they have to change. They can't stay near Jesus and continue behaving that way.

Necessary Food and Water

Grapes grow on vines. The branches of the grapevine get their food and water from the vine itself. Without that connection the branches will starve and there will be no grapes.

Jesus is the vine of life for His people. Staying connected to Him through prayer and reading your Bible is how you get nourishment.

Without Jesus you can't really do anything.

> "I am the vine; you are the branches. If you remain in Me and I in you, you will bear much fruit; apart from Me you can do nothing."
>
> John 15:5

Living It

Maya loves to help her grandma in the garden. They pull out weeds and even thin out the flowers that are too close together.

One of the things that makes Maya kind of sad is that when she picks a flower and takes it inside, it only lives a few days before dying. The flower gets no nourishment once it is cut off from the stem that gives it food. That why it's important to stay close to Jesus. Just like the flowers in their garden get food and water through their stem, as Maya keeps learning about Jesus and obeying Him, she will grow and serve Him.

Giving in Love

> "Go, sell everything you have and give to the poor, and you will have treasure in heaven. Then come, follow Me."
>
> Mark 10:21

A rich man came to Jesus and asked how he could have eternal life. Jesus' answer was consistent with what He always taught – love and care for others.

The foundation of life with Jesus is loving others. Jesus told the man to sell the things he owned and to use the money to help other people. That would show his unselfishness and care for others. That would give him treasure in heaven. Sadly, the rich man could not do it.

Living It

Christy has plenty of stuff: nice clothes, a computer, books. She has pretty much everything she wants. When she heard about kids who had nothing because an earthquake wrecked their homes, Christy had an idea.

She asked her mom to help and they had a garage sale. Christy sold some of her clothes and things and sent the money to ministries working to help kids in the earthquake area. This is loving others. That's what it's all about.

No Testing Allowed

Satan was tempting Jesus. He was trying to get Jesus to turn away from God and worship him.

Satan offered some pretty cool things to try to tempt Jesus, but none of them worked. Jesus turned away every temptation by quoting Scripture.

One of Satan's temptations was to challenge Scripture – to make Jesus prove that God would do what He said He would do. Jesus' response was this Scripture verse – don't test God. He doesn't have to prove anything to you.

> "It is also written:
> 'Do not put the
> Lord your God
> to the test.'"
>
> Matthew 4:7

Living It

Testing God is a big temptation, isn't it? Do you ever secretly pray, "God, if You really love me then do this or that … "? However you end that sentence, it ends up being a test for God to pass.

If you feel the need to put God to the test, it may mean that you don't really trust Him or His love for you. It's hard sometimes not to give in to this temptation because you may just want to "feel" His love. But, instead of testing Him, just remember all He has done for you and all the ways He shows you His love.

Lighting the Way

"You are the light
of the world.
A town built on a hill
cannot be hidden."

Matthew 5:14

Jesus called Himself the Light of the world, so it only makes sense that His followers are also light in a dark world.

The world is dark because of sin – the selfish, mean and bad things that people do. The light that comes from Jesus' love and righteousness reveals those bad things.

Jesus tells His followers that because they follow Him, they radiate His light in a dark world. They should never try to hide that light, because it leads to God and His love.

Living It

Sometimes Carol is tempted to just keep quiet about the fact that she is a Christian. Some of the kids she knows just make fun of her for talking about God.

But she has noticed that when she is around those same kids, they are a bit more careful about the language they use and the things they say. Carol knows that it's because she is shining Jesus' light into a dark world. How cool is that?

Watch Your Words

The words that come out of your mouth say a lot about what thoughts are racing through your mind. They also reveal your opinion of who Jesus is.

These words of Jesus are right in the middle of His famous Sermon on the Mount. It gave many instructions on how to live in a way that honors God. The bottom line is, watch your language. It says a lot about you.

> "I tell you, do not swear an oath at all: either by heaven, for it is God's throne; or by the earth, for it is His footstool; or by Jerusalem, for it is the city of the Great King."
>
> Matthew 5:34-35

Living It

Some of Maggie's friends aren't Christians. So she has the opportunity to be Jesus' light to them. It's hard because Maggie hears them using God's name as a swear word.

Maggie has to be careful that she doesn't pick up that habit just from hearing it so often. She doesn't want to disrespect God and she doesn't want to do anything to damage her influence for God.

Private Prayer

"When you pray, go into your room, close the door and pray to your Father, who is unseen. Then your Father, who sees what is done in secret, will reward you."

Matthew 6:6

Prayer is a very personal conversation, much like when you have a private talk with your best friend and you don't really want anyone else to know what you're talking about.

Personal prayer is between you and God. So, keep it private. Jesus says not to make a big show of praying in public about your personal and private requests.

Keep it between you and God. He will hear and He will answer.

Living It

Some people make a big show of life. They demand a lot of attention. They also do that when they pray. They use big, fancy words. Their voices are very dramatic and they pray with lots of emotion.

None of that means that God hears their prayers any more than any other people's. Jesus said prayer about your personal problems, fears and needs is between you and God. You don't have to make a big show of it. Just pray, alone, quietly. Then listen for God's answer.

Starting Small

Some people wait and pray for the opportunities to be important and influential people.

However, according to Jesus, no one gets big responsibilities before proving herself with small ones. It seems that Jesus is saying, "Show Me that I can trust you with small jobs and when you've proven yourself trustworthy and honest, then I'll give you bigger and more important jobs."

So, start small. Prove yourself. Move up.

> "Whoever can be trusted with very little can also be trusted with much, and whoever is dishonest with very little will also be dishonest with much."
>
> Luke 16:10

Living It

"Why can't I hang out with my friends at the mall?" Keira complained. "You just don't trust me." Mom shook her head sadly, "No, I'm afraid I don't, Keira. Remember, I gave you some freedom a few weeks ago and you didn't handle it well. You broke my simple rules, so now you have to earn my trust again."

Keira sighed. She remembered Jesus' words that proved Mom's point. Be trustworthy in small things and then be trusted with more!

Simple Belief

"Unless you people see signs and wonders," Jesus told him, "you will never believe."

John 4:48

It must have made Jesus sad that people wouldn't believe He was God's Son unless He did some big miracle for them. Jesus just wants people to love Him because He is God's Son and because He loved them first.

It is a human trait that getting stuff makes us believe that we are loved more easily than just hearing or reading "God loves you."

Living It

"What did you bring me?" Kyrah asked. Her mom was just home from a business trip and before saying, "I missed you or I love you," Kyrah wanted to know what she got. Kyrah's question made Mom feel as though Kyrah would love her more if she brought her a big, expensive gift.

Sadly, Kyrah approached God the same way with a "What will You do for me today?" attitude. Too bad. She was missing the basic message of the Bible. God loves you, Kyrah!

Follow Me

Two simple words. Many childhood games are made up of the idea of following someone and doing what the leader does. It's not a big deal, is it? Nope, except when it is.

The truth is that in real life pretty much everyone follows somebody. Either because she wants to be popular or accepted or considered successful in some way.

Jesus knew that people are followers so He made it simple – follow Him. That's what leads to peace and happiness.

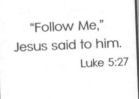

"Follow Me,"
Jesus said to him.
Luke 5:27

Living It

Maddie is kind of a loner. She doesn't have a lot of friends and she doesn't hang out with any particular group of kids. But she notices things. Things like all the girls who hang out with Colleen dress the same way, like the same things and are nice to some people and mean to others – all of them.

Maddie has decided that if she is going to try to be like anyone, it won't be someone like Colleen or any of the other "leaders". She will be like Jesus. She will follow Him.

Loving Others

> "I ask you, which is lawful on the Sabbath: to do good or to do evil, to save life or to destroy it?"
>
> Luke 6:9

Have you ever wondered if Jesus got tired of the nagging of the Pharisees? They were great rule-makers and insistent that everyone live by their rules.

What got lost in their world of rules was love and concern for other people, something that was always forefront in Jesus' mind. He cared about people, not man-made rules.

Living It

Jana watched her grandma very closely. Well, she noticed how Grandma lived. Jana noticed that sometimes Grandma didn't get all her housework done because she was chatting with the man next door whose wife just died.

Grandma missed church once in a while because the single mom down the street needed help with her three kids. Jana figures Grandma is a good example of loving others and not being stuck to a set of rules. Jana wants to be like Grandma.

Hear, Believe and Live

Jesus clearly stated that there is only one pathway to eternal life.

Many times He encouraged His followers to listen to His teachings, believe in God's love and accept Him as their Savior. That's the only path to heaven and eternal life. Some people try to say there is another way, but there is not.

There is only one way: Jesus.

"Very truly I tell you, whoever hears My word and believes Him who sent Me has eternal life and will not be judged but has crossed over from death to life."

John 5:24

Living It

Some people look for the easy way to do things. Some people cheat to take shortcuts to finish projects. There's no way to do either when it comes to having eternal life in heaven.

No shortcuts. No way other than trusting Jesus and believing in Him. Kelly learned that when she was just six years old and has been gently sharing that good news with her friends ever since. Jesus is the only way!

Parties in Heaven

"'For this son of mine was dead and is alive again; he was lost and is found.' So they began to celebrate."

Luke 15:24

Jesus said this as He told the story of the Prodigal Son – a story of a boy who disrespected his father and left home. The boy spent all his money. He was homeless and had nothing left. When he decided to go home and ask his father to give him a job, and not even to treat him as a son anymore, the father welcomed him home and celebrated that his son was home!

That's exactly what happens when a person accepts Jesus as Savior – a party in heaven!

Living It

Jana remembers when her 18-year-old brother got so mad at Mom and Dad that he left home and no one heard from him for a long time. Then one day he showed up at the front door.

Jana wondered if Mom and Dad would kick him out or punish him for all the worry he caused. But, they didn't. They celebrated that he was home again because they loved him. Jana knows that God's love is the same way. He welcomes sinners who accept Jesus as Savior. Parties in heaven ... for you!

No Judging!

The foundation of Jesus' teaching is love – loving God and loving others. It's not possible to criticize or judge someone if you're busy loving them.

Too often judging comes before loving, because some people think others should live by their rules. When people don't live by those rules, they are judged to be "bad Christians" or even "unsavory" people. Don't judge others because, if you do, Jesus says you will be judged yourself ... by God.

> "Do not judge, or you too will be judged."
> Matthew 7:1

Living It

"Moira is so stuck up. She thinks she is better than all of us," Bekah complained to Sarah. "Yeah, and she is bossy and rude, too," Sarah added.

Bekah and Sarah are judging Moira when they don't really know her. Maybe she isn't stuck up. Maybe she is shy. They should stop judging her and give her a chance after getting to know her. Otherwise, they will answer to God for judging Moira.

Secret Kindnesses

> "Be careful not to practice your righteousness in front of others, to be seen by them. If you do, you will have no reward from your Father in heaven."
>
> Matthew 6:1

Jesus warned His followers against doing good things for show. That means not doing good things just so other people see you do them and then, hopefully, think good things about you.

It doesn't matter what other people think. It only matters what Jesus thinks. He doesn't look at your showy acts. He looks at your heart to see whether or not you are truly compassionate and kind to others.

Living It

Bella did a lot of nice things for other people. She collected canned goods for the food pantry. She tutored in an after-school program. She ran errands for an elderly neighbor. Nice things.

The problem is that Bella made sure **everyone** knew about her nice acts. She bragged about them constantly to her friends and neighbors. So, according to Jesus' words, Bella was getting her reward right now – not when she stood before God in heaven.

Keep Your Focus

Jesus knew why He was on earth. He left the glory of heaven to come to earth as a human because He and God had a plan. Their plan was to have relationships with people. This made it possible for us to know God and to one day be in heaven with Him.

Jesus didn't let pressure from other people distract Him from what He came to do. He was focused.

> "Let us go somewhere else – to the nearby villages – so I can preach there also. That is why I have come."
>
> Mark 1:38

Living It

Leila is only twelve years old, but she has already felt God's call to serve Him as a missionary in a foreign country. She is a talented musician and some people try to convince her that she should be a professional musician or a music teacher.

But Leila keeps her focus on the calling God has given her. She will go to the mission field, unless He tells her something different.

Doing the Work of God

> "The work of God is this: to believe in the One He has sent."
>
> John 6:29

Some men came to Jesus and asked what they had to do in order to do the works that God required.

Jesus had an answer – a simple one. He said they just needed to believe in Him, believe that God sent Jesus and that He is God's Son. Now, that may sound pretty basic. But, the truth is, if you really believe that Jesus is God's Son then you will want to know Him, obey Him, and love Him. It won't be something you can fake.

Love and obedience comes from your heart.

Living It

Sadie goes to church and for all practical purposes appears to be a solid Jesus-follower. Except that, in the privacy of her own room, Sadie seldom reads her Bible because she just doesn't care what it says. She very seldom prays because she doesn't really believe that God answers prayer.

Sadie doesn't think about salvation because she doesn't really believe Jesus is God's Son or that He came to live, teach, die and come back to life because of His powerful love for her.

Repent Now!

Jesus had a singular purpose for coming to earth. You see, humans had no chance of knowing God personally because the sin of mankind was a barrier between God and man.

Jesus came to teach about God's love but also to die – to pay the penalty for people's sin – your sin. So, His call is to repent – to turn away from sin – to **stop** sinning while they still had time.

"Repent, for the kingdom of heaven has come near."
Matthew 4:17

Living It

OK, let's be honest. You're a kid and you've got your whole life ahead of you to focus on being serious about living for God. Why not just enjoy life now and do what you want?

There's a good reason. Jesus said that the kingdom of heaven is near. No one knows when Jesus will come back to take people to heaven. Repent now and spend your life loving and serving Him!

May

Celebrate!

"How can the guests of the bridegroom fast while he is with them? They cannot, so long as they have him with them."

Mark 2:19

When someone throws a big party, like a wedding for example, the guests are invited to celebrate with the host.

It wouldn't make sense for the guests to come to the party and refuse to celebrate because they are on a diet or something. They can go on a diet after the party.

Jesus encouraged people to live lives filled with love for God and others, especially while He was on earth with them.

Living It

Some Christians have a "doom and gloom" approach to life. They look at the negatives of the sin in the world or the people who choose to outwardly turn away from God.

Jesus encouraged His followers to pay attention to His love for them and for everyone, and to celebrate all the wonderful things He has given. Of course, we should pray for those who don't know Him and share His love with them. But don't forget to celebrate Jesus!

Hanging Out with the Sick

When Jesus walked on earth the religious leaders criticized Him for spending time with "sinners".

They didn't believe that they were sinners, too. They thought Jesus should just hang out with them – the religious leaders. He shouldn't rub shoulders with people who didn't believe in God or people who did bad things. Jesus disagreed, because if the religious leaders had faith all figured out, they didn't need Him.

But, those who didn't understand God needed Him.

> "It is not the healthy who need a doctor, but the sick."
> Luke 5:31

Living It

Tricia is intentional. That means that she does things on purpose. One of those things was joining a choir so she had the chance to get to know other kids who were not Christians.

She didn't just hang out with her Christian friends, though she did spend time with them, too. Tricia wanted to get to know kids with whom she could share God's love. That's what Jesus did.

From Darkness to Light

"I have come into the world as a light, so that no one who believes in Me should stay in darkness."

John 12:46

You know what it's like to walk into a dark, dark room. You might stub your toe on a chair you can't see or even walk into a wall. You just can't see what's going on.

But even a small light reveals what is in the darkness. Jesus is light like that. He reveals the evil and sin in your heart.

Meeting Jesus is like turning on a light in your heart.

Living It

Debbie is jealous. She won't admit it, but she is jealous of her friend Kayla because Debbie is a good singer, but Kayla is an awesome singer! Debbie pretends to cheer Kayla on, but in her heart she secretly wants Kayla to mess up the words of her songs.

But when Debbie kneels down to pray one night, Jesus turns on a light in her heart and she sees the sin there. Jesus' light motivates Debbie to ask forgiveness and His help in celebrating Kayla's successes.

Who Cares?

Jesus knew that people worry about all kinds of things. For example, some girls worry about having clothes with the "right" designer's label. Those girls can be pretty mean to the ones who don't have them.

Jesus wants you to know that there are more important things than what you are wearing or even what you're eating and drinking. Trust Him – that is the most important.

> "I tell you, do not worry about your life, what you will eat or drink; or about your body, what you will wear. Is not life more than food, and the body more than clothes?"
> Matthew 6:25

Living It

Erica dreads riding the school bus, because she feels trapped when she is on it. There are some girls on the bus who are just mean. They pick on her about what she's wearing. "Your clothes look like baby clothes," is their favorite line.

Erica's family doesn't have a lot of money so she can't have fancy clothes. But the cool thing is that Erica trusts Jesus' words. Life is more than what you wear. It's more important to be close to Jesus and to be serving Him. It doesn't really matter what those bus girls say!

Judge and Be Judged

"In the same way you judge others, you will be judged, and with the measure you use, it will be measured to you."

Matthew 7:2

Wow, it's so easy to be critical of other people, isn't it? Too often we judge people who don't believe exactly what we think they should. We judge people who don't behave the way we think they should.

Jesus' words remind us that judging others is not our business. God is the only one who should judge. When you are tempted to judge other people, just remember that you will be judged by the same standard you use – and your judge is God.

Living It

"Brody gets away with murder," Kaiya complained to her mother. She felt like Brody constantly disobeyed their parents and got away without doing his chores. Not that she didn't try to get out of her chores every once in a while, but she was glad to point out Brody's failures!

Whew, Kaiya needs to remember that as she points things out to Mom, the same standards will be used to judge her, too.

Two of Jesus' followers came to Him and asked Him if He would do whatever they wanted. Jesus didn't just dismiss them or tell them to go away. He asked them what they wanted.

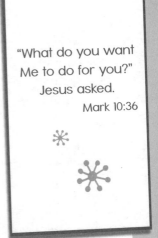

"What do you want Me to do for you?" Jesus asked.

Mark 10:36

Why? Because Jesus cares about your feelings. He cares about what you want. He cares about your needs. He's willing to listen to what you ask, even if what you ask for isn't good for you.

Living It

Sometimes it feels like the world is crashing down around you. Marsha knows how that feels. Her grandma is super sick. Her dad lost his job. Her mom is working full-time and trying to take care of Grandma and encourage her dad.

"Doesn't Jesus care about us?" she wondered. He does. He wants to know what she wants Him to do for her. She just needs to tell Him.

Peace All Around

"Peace be with you."
Luke 24:36

Jesus' followers were very sad. He had been murdered and they didn't understand, because they believed He was God's Son and, well, how could He be dead?

They were afraid that the same people who killed Him would come after them, too. Many of them stayed together and tried to stay out of sight. They didn't know what was going to happen now, without Jesus.

But then, in the quietness of the little room they were in, suddenly Jesus was there with them, alive, and giving them peace.

Living It

Sadness settles in your heart and kind of takes over your emotions and attitudes. Everything you do is under the blanket of sadness. Lara knows that. She is sad because her dad has moved out. She misses him.

She's kind of scared about what's going to happen to her and her brother and even to her mom. It makes her feel better when Mom reminds her that Jesus will give her peace. He knows what's happening and He will take care of all of them.

Special Powers

Jesus' work on earth was finished. He had been murdered, but God brought Him back to life. Now He was going back to heaven.

But, there was still work to be done on earth. There were still people who needed to hear about God's love for them. There were still people who needed to be encouraged to repent of their sins and turn to God.

Jesus told His followers to wait for the Holy Spirit to come. He would live in their hearts and help them do Jesus' work all over the earth.

> "You will receive power when the Holy Spirit comes on you; and you will be My witnesses in Jerusalem, and in all Judea and Samaria, and to the ends of the earth."
>
> Acts 1:8

Living It

Joan is serious about serving Jesus. But the thought of actually speaking to someone about her faith is scary. Yeah, very scary.

So, knowing that the Holy Spirit is living in her heart to give her God's power to do His work is really special! It helps her be brave and it excites her to be able to do God's work!

Mercy

"Blessed are the merciful, for they will be shown mercy."

Matthew 5:7

Much of Jesus' teaching is about how people get along with each other and how people treat each other. These words were spoken as part of His Sermon on the Mount in a section known as the Beatitudes.

Jesus pointed out that people who show mercy, which is forgiveness, love and patience to others, will be shown mercy by God.

So, treat others the way you want to be treated. Pay attention to others.

Living It

Olivia teases Charlotte all the time. She picks on her every chance she gets and it doesn't matter if there are other people around or not.

One day at school Olivia tripped and dropped her lunch tray and spilled food everywhere. Charlotte could have laughed and made fun of her. But she didn't. She helped Olivia pick up her tray and even shared her own food with her. This is showing mercy.

Anger-Free Living

Why can't people just get along? Jesus focused a lot of His teaching on how people should treat each other.

Some people justify their actions by saying things like, "Well, I've never murdered anyone so I'm not a bad person." But look, Jesus brought His teaching down to the simple statement of "Don't be angry." You will be judged for that. Try to get along with others. That's so important.

It's how you show love to others – your love and God's love.

> "I tell you that anyone who is angry with a brother or sister will be subject to judgment."
> Matthew 5:22

Living It

Whoa. This is kind of a scary statement, isn't it? Can you honestly say that you've never even been angry with another person?

Yeah, we all have been angry at one time or another. Jesus encourages us to make things right with people and settle our differences so we can resolve our anger and be at peace with others.

Storing Up Treasures

"Do not store up for yourselves treasures on earth, where moths and vermin destroy, and where thieves break in and steal."

Matthew 6:19

Some people live their lives focused on money. They work to get more and more money, sometimes hurting the people they work with by their actions. They want more and more stuff – a nicer car, bigger house, fancier gadgets. Jesus warns that this is the wrong focus.

What you have here on earth is not nearly so important once you realize that it all will be gone one day. Your things will get old, break, or even be stolen. One day you will leave this earth for heaven or hell and none of that stuff you've worked so hard to get can go with you.

Living It

Talia's parents started teaching her an important lesson when she was very young. That lesson is: Money does not buy happiness. Sometimes it's hard because Talia would like to have an iPad or smartphone or any of the other nice things some of her friends have.

But the fact is her parents can't afford those things, and that's OK. They are generous with their time and money in serving God and supporting His work around the world. They are storing up treasures, just not here on earth.

Heavenly Treasures

What did Jesus mean here? He had just said not to store up treasures on earth, now He says to store them in heaven instead.

How do you deposit money in heaven? Well, the treasures Jesus was talking about have nothing to do with money. Treasures in heaven are deposited by serving God, loving Him, serving others and helping them, supporting those who do God's work around the world and just generally doing the things that matter to God.

That's heavenly treasure.

> "Store up for yourselves treasures in heaven, where moths and vermin do not destroy, and where thieves do not break in and steal."
>
> Matthew 6:20

Living It

Some people might say that Jenny and her family are poor, and by the financial standards of most people, they are. They don't own a home, have the latest clothes or gadgets and their car is over 10 years old.

But they are missionaries in Africa and their lives are devoted to helping the people there who are sick and sharing the message of God's love with them. They are rich in the love of God and people, and in the knowledge that they are doing what God wants them to do.

Where Is Your Heart?

"For where your treasure is, there your heart will be also."

Matthew 6:21

Jesus just came right out and said that whatever is most important to you is what you will care about most. So, if your goal is to make lots of money then that's what your heart will focus on – that's what you will care about most.

You may say you care about things like people not having clean water to drink, or the HIV/Aids pandemic, but if your day-in and day-out goal is "make more money" and it's not for the purpose of helping those in need ... well, then your heart is not with others but only money.

Living It

Cindy does things to earn money. She does yard work for neighbors, takes her old clothing to resale shops, does extra chores that her parents pay her for. Cindy's goal is to buy herself an iPad.

Laura also does things to earn money. She does a lot of the same jobs Cindy does. Laura has a goal, too. She wants to send money to an organization that is helping provide fresh water for poor people.

Two girls. Two "treasures". One for self, and one for others.

Forgive and Forgive

The bottom line here is that it is impossible to truly serve God without your relationships with people being affected.

When someone hurts you or cheats you, what do you want to do? Hurt them back? Are you willing to forgive them? If you don't forgive those who hurt you, do you still expect God to forgive you when you sin against Him?

Forgive others ... it's the God-way!

"If you forgive other people when they sin against you, your heavenly Father will also forgive you."
Matthew 6:14

Living It

Dorie is so mad at Anna that she could scream! They have been best friends since second grade. But then Anna decided to be best friends with Abbie and Dorie was hurt and angry.

After a couple of weeks Anna wanted to be friends again. Dorie could refuse to forgive Anna, but she doesn't. She remembers what Jesus said about forgiveness so she quickly forgives Anna and they are friends again!

God's Constant Care

> "Look at the birds of the air; they do not sow or reap or store away in barns, and yet your heavenly Father feeds them. Are you not much more valuable than they?"
>
> Matthew 6:26

Think about this statement. Think about how God takes care of birds by making sure they have food.

Birds don't have jobs. Birds don't have barns in which to store food in, but each day God provides what birds and other animals need in order to survive. God loves the creatures He created.

More good news: He loves you even more than the animals He made. He will take even better care of you!

Living It

Now think about this: God loves you so much He promises to take care of you and supply you with everything you need. There is a difference between the things you want and the things you need.

Don't think this means He will give you whatever you want. Take a minute and thank God right now for providing your needs. Thank Him for His wonderful love.

True Belief

Two blind men followed Jesus and called out to Him to help them. He stopped and asked them if they really believed that He could restore their sight.

This question is so important. Why would Jesus help someone who didn't really believe in His power? It was a simple question, but if the men answered honestly (and who would lie to Jesus?) then their lives could be changed forever.

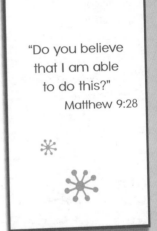

"Do you believe
that I am able
to do this?"
Matthew 9:28

Living It

Do you believe that Jesus is really able to answer your prayers? Think about the things you ask Him to do. Are there some big things, like healing a sick person, finding a real friend or getting a new job for Dad?

Do you really, honestly believe that Jesus can and will answer your prayers? If you don't believe Him, why would He answer your prayers?

Growing Faith

> "If you have faith as small as a mustard seed, you can say to this mulberry tree, 'Be uprooted and planted in the sea,' and it will obey you."
>
> Luke 17:6

First of all – a mustard seed is a really, really tiny seed. So, Jesus is saying that just a tiny bit of faith gives you the power to do amazing things.

What is faith? It is believing and trusting that God is real; that Jesus is God's only Son, who died for your sins and was raised back to life by the power of God. Do you really, truly, honestly believe?

The point is that the object (in this case a tree) obeys faith because everything, absolutely everything is under God's power.

Living It

Jill wants to believe in God's power and in His love for her, but it's hard. Sometimes in the middle of the night she wonders if God really loves her and if He really hears her prayers.

Faith is something that grows. So, Jill will learn that having a little faith and seeing God answer her prayers leads to more faith so she can trust Him for bigger things. You will learn that, too. Faith grows and grows as you see God work.

Doing What's Hard

When Jesus prays these words He knows that He is about to be arrested, tortured and eventually killed, even though He has never done a wrong thing in His life. He would go through all of that simply because of His love for you.

It's kind of scary to face things that are hard – even for Jesus. What's cool about this prayer is that Jesus says, "OK, I'll do it, God, because it is what You want." He obeyed and trusted God to get Him through it.

> "My Father, if it is not possible for this cup to be taken away unless I drink it, may Your will be done."
> Matthew 26:42

Living It

Cora's family is moving to a different town hundreds of miles from where she has always lived. She is scared. She doesn't want to go, but she doesn't have a choice because her dad got a new job and they have to move.

Cora knows that her mom and dad pray about every decision they make and that they always ask God to do what's best for the family. So, this move must be God's will. Knowing that, Cori decides to try to make the best of it and even to be excited about the new friends she will eventually meet.

Be Careful!

> "Watch and pray so that you will not fall into temptation. The spirit is willing, but the flesh is weak."
>
> Matthew 26:41

Temptation is going to come. There is no doubt about it. Every person will be tempted in some way. Jesus warns you to be careful and to use the tools you have available to avoid temptation.

Watch, which means pay attention to what you're thinking and doing. And pray, because your strength to resist temptation comes from staying close to God and you do that by prayer.

You can try by yourself to resist temptation but honestly, you're not strong enough by yourself.

Living It

Ariana has some friends who don't care a bit about living for God. She knows that they have no respect for God, for the Bible or for Christians.

But Ariana is overconfident. She thinks that by her own power she can resist the temptation to do the things they do and think the way they think.

But she's wrong. She needs to ask God to help her and she must be careful about falling into the temptation to join their attitudes and actions. Be careful!

God's Justice

Jesus' message of love for others is consistent. Even if someone does something terrible to you, if you can find it in your heart to forgive her and give her another chance, then you are being like Jesus.

So, don't fight with people who do mean things to you. Instead, show Christ's love by not reacting. Just keep on being kind, kind, kind.

Let God take care of all "getting even" things. It's not your problem.

> "I tell you, do not resist an evil person. If anyone slaps you on the right cheek, turn to them the other cheek."
>
> Matthew 5:39

Living It

Jenna knows this verse. She's heard before that she should turn the other cheek. But why? There's this girl at school that picks on her every chance she gets. She is downright mean.

Why should Jenna give her a chance to hurt her more? Simple. Because Jesus says, "Be nice. Take whatever is tossed at you. I'll take care of justice." OK. Jenna gets it. She doesn't react, even when she wants to. She trusts Jesus to take care of things.

Faith of a Child

> "Let the little
> children come to
> Me, and do not
> hinder them, for
> the kingdom of
> heaven belongs to
> such as these."
>
> Matthew 19:14

Isn't this cool? Jesus loves children. When His disciples wanted to shoo children away so they wouldn't bother Jesus, He stopped them. He even gave children a big compliment by saying that everyone should have faith like a child. What does that mean?

We should have faith that trusts Jesus and takes Him at His word. Don't complicate faith in Jesus by challenging everything He says. Trust His actions and His promises.

Living It

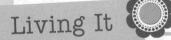

Kelly is known as the Question Queen around her house. She has questions about pretty much everything, except when it comes to her relationship with Jesus.

Well sure, she has questions about things like what Bible verses actually mean or what Jesus wants her to do with her life. But she doesn't ever question whether or not Jesus loves her. She never wonders if the Bible is true or if God is real. She believes what Jesus says – every word.

The Greatest Gift

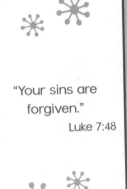

When a sinful woman came to a home where Jesus was, people were amazed that Jesus paid her any attention. But, by the way she treated Him, Jesus knew that she believed He was God's Son and she had true faith in Him.

Jesus' response to her was to forgive her sins so she could have a friendship with Him and look forward to being in heaven with Him some day.

Forgiving sins is the greatest gift Jesus gives.

"Your sins are forgiven."

Luke 7:48

Living It

It's hard for Lucy to have good feelings about herself. No one has ever told her that she is a good girl. No one says anything nice about her. She has only been told about the bad things she does.

When Lucy heard that Jesus loves her, she had trouble believing it. She wondered how He could love her when she does such bad things. Bible stories like this one prove to her that Jesus loves her and that He forgives her sins. She is a good girl and beautiful in His sight.

Jesus Means What He Says

"Let's go over to the other side of the lake."

Luke 8:22

Jesus said this to His disciples just before they got into a boat and started across the lake. As soon as they set sail, Jesus fell asleep.

While He was sleeping, a storm grew and the disciples became scared that the boat would sink. They woke Jesus to save them. He said, "Where is your faith?" Why did He say that? Well, the trip started with these words, "Let's go over to the other side of the lake." He didn't say, "Let's go half way and then sink." They were Jesus' closest friends, but they didn't really trust Him.

Living It

Linnie trusts Jesus ... sort of. When life gets scary, then her trust gets shaky. She is learning, though, that Jesus says what He means and He means what He says.

So, just as Jesus meant it when He told His disciples they were going to the other side of the lake, He means it when He says He loves Linnie and will take care of her. She is learning to trust His heart. Every time she trusts a little bit more and sees Him take care of her, she trusts more the next time.

Doing the Right Thing

People who try to live the way Jesus teaches make other people un-comfortable.

And, when people are un-comfortable they might get a little prickly toward the people who make them feel awkward. That leads to a kind of persecution – being picked on because you treat others with kindness, are honest and fair.

Living the way Jesus teaches is best. Never fear, though, He knows what is happening and He will bless you for choosing to obey Him.

> "Blessed are those who are persecuted because of righteousness, for theirs is the kingdom of heaven."
>
> Matthew 5:10

Living It

Melea doesn't say bad things about other girls. Her heart is very tender and she knows it would hurt their feelings if they heard bad things about themselves.

However, some of her friends enjoy ripping off other girls for their clothing choices or how well they do in school or if they are any good at sports – pretty much any reason they can find. Melea doesn't join in their conversation so now they make fun of her, too! She doesn't care, though. She knows she is behaving in a way that Jesus likes.

Jesus Will Take Care of You

> "Blessed are you when people insult you, persecute you and falsely say all kinds of evil against you because of Me."
>
> Matthew 5:11

Most people are looking out for Number One – themselves. So, when a person feels her success or popularity is threatened by another person, the human thing is to strike out and try to hurt that person.

Jesus said that people might hurt you just because you love and serve Him. He said it would be OK. You will be blessed if people hurt you because of your faith in Him.

Remember to stay close to Jesus and He will take care of you.

Living It

Lisa loves Jesus. She cares about obeying Him. She does her best to serve Him. It's not always easy, but she tries. A lot of her friends love and serve Him, too, and that's great.

However, she has some friends who do not love Jesus. Sometimes they make fun of Lisa, calling her names and saying that the way she lives is lame.

But it doesn't bother Lisa. It just proves to her that she is living the right way. She knows Jesus is happy with her and that's all that really matters.

Give Up on Worry

People worry over things that have already happened; things that are happening; things that might happen.

Most of the stuff people worry about is stuff that they have no control over so worrying about it will not change a single thing.

What's the solution to worry? God. Yep, keep God's love in the center of your heart. So, when you start worrying about something, just stop and say, "No. I'm not going to worry about this.

I'm going to give it to God and let Him take care of it." Do that every day, because every day has its own troubles.

> "Do not worry about tomorrow, for tomorrow will worry about itself. Each day has enough trouble of its own."
>
> Matthew 6:34

Living It

Anna is starting a new school in the Fall. She's very nervous, because she won't know anyone and will not have any friends. She worries about making new friends. In fact, she worries about it so much that she can't sleep at night.

Mom gently reminds her that worrying about it won't help. They begin to pray together every night, asking God to help Anna be friendly and to make new friends quickly. Anna feels better knowing that God is handling the situation.

Personal Decisions

> "Not everyone who says to Me, 'Lord, Lord,' will enter the kingdom of heaven, but only the one who does the will of My Father who is in heaven."
>
> Matthew 7:21

Have you noticed that some people speak God's name, but seem to have no clue who He really is? They aren't really interested in serving Him and they don't love Him. They don't even think about Him much, except maybe when they have a problem.

Jesus says those people shouldn't expect to go to heaven. The people who go to heaven to live with Him are the ones who obey and follow Him.

Living It

Rachel's parents are Christians and they take Rachel and her brother to church every week. Rachel usually sits with her friends and daydreams or writes notes during the service. She doesn't think much about God.

Rachel just assumes that when the time comes she will go to heaven just because her parents are Christians. She thinks that's enough, but it isn't. Becoming a Christian is a personal choice and must be made individually. Loving, serving and obeying God is the only way to get to heaven.

A Firm Foundation

If you've seen news reports about floods, you know that cars, barns, trees and houses can be swept away in powerful water, especially houses that are not built on firm foundations like rock. The rock won't wash away so the house built on it is safer.

Jesus says that people who hear His teaching, obey it and put it into practice in their lives are wise – just like the man who built his house on rock instead of a muddy hillside!

"Everyone who hears these words of Mine and puts them into practice is like a wise man who built his house on the rock. The rain came down, the streams rose, and the winds blew and beat against that house; yet it did not fall, because it had its foundation on the rock."
Matthew 7:24-25

Living It

Jillian has heard these Scripture verses before and she always wonders what it has to do with her. This is how: if Jillian puts more importance on what her friends think than on what God thinks, then she is building her house on a muddy slope instead of on rock.

Making God and His Word the most important means Jillian is building her life on a strong foundation.

What Makes You Unclean?

"Are you so dull?" He asked. "Don't you see that nothing that enters a person from the outside can defile them'?"

Mark 7:18

What is Jesus saying? Just that nothing you eat or put in your body makes you sin. Sin comes from the heart.

When you decide in your heart to be mean to someone or to cheat while playing a game or taking a test, that is a sin.

When you choose to tell a lie or do anything else that is disobedient to how Jesus teaches you to live, then your heart is unclean.

Living It

Meredith has a bad temper. She knows that she does. She knows that she needs to keep it under control.

Sometimes her brother makes her so mad that she decides to just let him have it! She yells and screams at him and even tries to hit him. Meredith can blame her brother all she wants, but the truth is that she chooses to let her temper blast. It comes from inside her.

Loving Everyone

This is awesome! Jesus challenges His followers to go beyond the friendship line.

Be nice to your enemies – people who are not nice to you. Help them in any way you can. Don't worry about getting even.

Be even kinder and more helpful to them than you are to your friends. That will show that you are a follower of God, because He is also kind to those who do not love Him.

> "Love your enemies, do good to them, and lend to them without expecting to get anything back. Then your reward will be great, and you will be sons of the Most High, because He is kind to the ungrateful and wicked."
>
> Luke 6:35

Living It

OK, let's be honest. It's easy and even fun being nice to your friends. It's fun to do extra nice things for them and to surprise them with special things. But enemies – people who are mean to you or tell lies about you – yeah, it's not so much fun to be nice to them, is it?

But it is what Jesus says. After all, anyone can be nice to her friends. But being nice to your enemies – now, that shows you are a Jesus-follower!

No-Rules Living

"God did not send His Son into the world to condemn the world, but to save the world through Him."

John 3:17

Some people think that following Jesus actually means following a long list of rules. That's not true.

Jesus' teachings on how to treat other people, how to treat God, and the right way to live are not just rules to make life hard.

If followed, they will make life more pleasant, relationships better and the world a better place.

Living It

Julie knows that God loves her. She completely believes that. Since she trusts His love, Julie never looks at the teachings of Jesus as rules to be kept. They are guidelines to help her treat others with kindness and respect.

She knows that Jesus did come to make the world a better place. If everyone lived the way Jesus taught, the world would be a much safer and happier place.

June

Something In Your Eye

"How can you say to your brother, 'Let me take the speck out of your eye,' when all the time there is a plank in your own eye?"

Matthew 7:4

Jesus knows that some people are very critical of others. Often they pick on issues that are similar to problems they have – to an even greater degree.

Jesus asks how you can pick on someone for doing something that you yourself do.

Take care of your own problems before telling someone else to fix theirs.

Living It

Phoebe complains about how Ella is so judgmental. "She picks on other girls about just about everything!" Phoebe says. She isn't exactly right, but Ella is a little critical of others.

However, Phoebe is way more critical of others. But she doesn't see that in herself. She needs to read Jesus' words here and take them to heart.

First Things First

Keep your relationships healthy. Jesus is saying that God cares about how you and your friends and family get along.

So, if someone is mad at you – whether you did anything wrong or not – work it out. Apologize if you need to; clear up misunderstandings; give in if you're being stubborn. Just make sure you and your friend or family member are OK.

Once those relationships are good, then give your gifts to God. Don't expect Him to bless you if you aren't doing your part to keep relationships healthy.

> "If you are offering your gift at the altar and there remember that your brother or sister has something against you, leave your gift there in front of the altar. First go and be reconciled to them; then come and offer your gift."
>
> Matthew 5:23-24

Living It

Sammie is super mad at Mia. But Mia doesn't have a clue as to why, so she just ignores Sammie. Mia goes on with life and does everything as usual. But as she settles down to have a devotional time with God, this verse pops into her mind.

She thinks, "Maybe I should find out why Sammie is so mad at me." She asks to talk to Sammie, and discovers it was all a big misunderstanding. Once they talk it through, they are good friends once more. Now Mia can read her Bible and pray, knowing that her friendship with Sammie is healthy again.

Go the Extra Mile

"If you love those who love you, what reward will you get? Are not even the tax collectors doing that? And if you greet only your own people, what are you doing more than others? Do not even pagans do that?"

Matthew 5:46-47

Evidence that a girl's heart belongs to Jesus is seen in how she treats other people.

Any girl is nice to her friends, whether she knows Jesus or not. But to be nice to people you don't know – that's going the extra mile.

It may be scary to talk to someone you don't know but it shows that Jesus is in your heart, filling it with love for all – friends you know and friends you don't yet know.

Living It

Erica is the "new girl." In a small town with a smallish school, everyone knows that she is new and that she doesn't know anyone. Most of the kids just ignore her and kind of look right past her as if she is invisible.

Lisa is not like the other kids, though. She breaks away from her group of friends, introduces herself to Erica and gets to know her. Yeah, it was scary to do that, but Lisa thought first about how scared Erica might be to not know anyone.

Honor and Respect

Jesus knows that some of us need things spelled out for us. We need to know exactly what He wants from us.

In this verse, Jesus begins teaching His followers how to pray. We should not begin our prayer times with requests or complaints or anything other than praise. Jesus taught us to recognize that God is our Father, our caregiver and we should honor His name.

Respect God's name above all others. Keep Him in a place of respect and honor as you begin your prayer time.

> "This, then, is how you should pray: 'Our Father in heaven, hallowed be Your name.'"
>
> Matthew 6:9

Living It

Some people pray with a heavy-duty case of the "Gimme's". "Dear God, give me this and do that for me. I want, I want, I want ..."

Jesus encouraged people to honor God before they begin asking for things. God is not to be viewed like a Santa type of being. He isn't here just to give you stuff. Honor Him. Respect Him. Trust Him. Recognize that He is God above all else.

Let God's Will Be done

> "Your kingdom come, Your will be done, on earth as it is in heaven."
> Matthew 6:10

This is the second line of what is known as the Lord's Prayer.

Jesus taught that after you recognize God as Father and honor His name, the next step is to be submissive to His will.

No, wait, not just submissive, but to actually ask that His will be done on earth, in your life, in the lives of people you love, everything around you. This request allows Him to be in control of earth, just as He is in heaven.

Living It

Roma loves God. Well, she says she does. She certainly goes to church. She reads her Bible and prays. But, she doesn't usually say, "Have things your way, God."

No, Roma tends to tell God what she wants Him to do. That is not what Jesus taught. He said to give up your own will and just tell God to take over and have things His way. Roma still has a few things to learn about a life of faith. She will.

Ask for What You Need

Jesus taught His followers the right way to pray. It's interesting that His model of prayer did not include a lot of requests for the person praying. His prayer model asks for just what you need for this day.

Jesus says to ask for the food you need for this day; the help you need for this day; the comfort and strength you need for this day – not tomorrow or next week or a year from now.

Trust God to meet your needs one day at a time.

"Give us today our daily bread."
Matthew 6:11

Living It

Annie's parents don't actually tell her when they don't have enough money, even for the basic things, but Annie can tell when they are worried. She hears their whispered conversations. She notices when Mom says, "Oh, I couldn't eat another bite" when she has hardly eaten anything but she pushes more food toward Annie and her sister. Annie could worry like crazy, but she doesn't. She just prays the way Jesus taught: "God, give us just what we need for today." She knows that tomorrow she can (and will) pray exactly that same prayer.

Forgiving to Be Forgiven

"Forgive us our debts, as we also have forgiven our debtors."

Matthew 6:12

These words are from the prayer Jesus taught His disciples, the Lord's Prayer.

He says we should ask God to forgive our debts and our sins, but not only that, we also must forgive those who sin against us. What does that mean? It means to forgive people who hurt you, cheat you, do mean things to you. How can you expect God to forgive you if you can't forgive others?

If you need help forgiving, ask God and He will help you.

Living It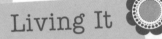

When Kyra asked God's forgiveness for her sins, a name popped into her mind – Abbie. "Ugh," was her reaction. Abbie used to be her best friend, but she dumped Kyra to be besties with Sara.

Each time Abbie's name popped into her thoughts, it was like Kyra heard Jesus saying, "Forgive her. Let it go." God eventually taught her that she needed to forgive Abbie because God forgave her sins. If God forgave her sins then she should forgive Abbie. It was the right thing to do.

No Temptation

The next step in Jesus' example of prayer is a request for help and protection.

Jesus will not tempt you to do bad things like lose your temper or hurt another person. Those things come from Satan. He sneaks into your mind and heart and encourages you to do bad things.

Jesus teaches us to pray that God will keep us away from Satan.

"Lead us not into temptation, but deliver us from the evil one."

Matthew 6:13

Living It

Satan is so sneaky. He knows where you are weak. It might be that your self-esteem is kind of low so he can sneak in there and pull you away from God by the things he gets you to say to yourself.

Satan doesn't have to do big showy things to get you to sin. It's the subtle, little things he does that trip you up. You can't fight him off by yourself, so be sure to ask God's help. Jesus said that is just what you should do!

Future Promise

> "My Father's house has many rooms; if it were not so, would I have told you that I am going there to prepare a place for you? And if I go and prepare a place for you, I will come back and take you to be with Me that you also may be where I am."
>
> John 14:2-3

Jesus was speaking to His disciples when He said these words. He was trying to prepare them for what was coming – His arrest and murder.

Jesus wanted His disciples to realize that none of what was going to happen to Him was in vain. He was making it possible for them to be able to join Him in heaven.

Jesus promises to come back to earth and get His followers so that they can be with Him in heaven. What a wonderful promise!

Living It

Ever since she first heard the stories of Jesus coming to earth, Debbie has felt terrible that He was treated so poorly. "Why did they hurt Him? Why did He have to die?" she wondered.

But, as her faith has grown, Debbie has come to understand the truths of these verses. Jesus and His Father had a plan to make it possible for sinful people to be able to go to heaven. He promises that we will be with Him. Now Debbie thanks Him every day for this wonderful promise.

The Way to Heaven

There have always been people who teach that there is another way to get to heaven, other than the way Jesus teaches. They are wrong.

Jesus made it very clear that the only way to heaven is to believe that He is God's Son, who died for your sins, and is now in heaven with God.

Accepting Jesus as Savior, confessing your sins to Him and inviting Him to live in your heart – that's the way, the truth and the life.

> "I am the way and the truth and the life. No one comes to the Father except through Me."
>
> John 14:6

Living It

Marta knows Jesus. Her friend Charlotte does not. Marta has tried many times to tell Charlotte about Jesus' love.

She has tried to explain that accepting Jesus is the only way to heaven. But Charlotte doesn't believe her. "If I live a good life and am kind and honest, then I'll get to heaven. That's all it takes," she says. She's wrong. She needs to read the verse and understand that Jesus is the only pathway to heaven.

Test of Love

> "Anyone who loves Me, will obey My teaching. My Father will love them, and we will come to them and make our home with them."
>
> John 14:23

You will often hear people who may not really know Him mention God's name.

Athletes thank God for their victories. People who have survived a crisis mention the "Big Guy" who watched out for them. These people might even say they love God.

But, Jesus said there is one true piece of evidence that people do love Him and that is obedience.

Knowing what Jesus teaches by reading the Bible and obeying His teachings – that shows real love for Him.

Living It

Kelly wonders why obedience shows love. "Isn't it possible that I do love Jesus, even if I don't always obey His teachings?" Maybe.

Everyone disobeys sometimes, because none of us are perfect. We disobey sometimes without really thinking about it. But making the effort to know what Jesus teaches and trying to obey – even asking His help in obeying – that shows that Jesus really matters to you and that you love Him enough to want to obey.

Seed on the Path

Jesus often told stories to teach His lessons. One story was about seeds that a farmer sowed.

Some of the seed fell on the path and Jesus explained that this example was of people who hear the Word of God – the truth – but don't immediately grab it with their hearts.

The devil is able to snatch the truth away so that they do not believe in Jesus.

> "A farmer went out to sow his seed. Some fell along the path; it was trampled on, and the birds ate it up. The seed is the Word of God. Those along the path are the ones who hear, and then the devil comes and takes away the Word from their hearts, so that they may not believe and be saved."
>
> Luke 8:5, 11-12

Living It

Lisa's mom has told her about Jesus' love. But Lisa hasn't believed it or accepted Jesus yet. It's OK to take time to think about it. But, while she is thinking she has thoughts like "maybe it isn't true" or "why would Jesus love me? I'm not special."

Yeah, Satan is trying to snatch the truth away from Lisa's heart. What should she do? She should talk with her mom and hear the truth again. Don't let Satan win, Lisa!

Faith with No Roots

> "Some fell on rocky ground, and when it came up, the plants withered because they had no moisture. Those on the rocky ground are the ones who receive the Word with joy when they hear it, but they have no root. They believe for a while, but in the time of testing they fall away."
>
> Luke 8:6, 13

This is the second example Jesus gave of seed that a farmer sows.

This seed fell on rocky ground and the plants died because their roots couldn't get water. That's like people who happily accept Jesus as Savior, but they don't grow by reading the Bible and spending time with God. So, when a crisis comes, they give up. They haven't gotten the "food" of God's Word to help them grow strong.

Living It

Growing a friendship takes time. The more time you spend with a friend, the better you get to know each other. That's just as true of friendship with Jesus as it is with people.

Get to know Jesus by reading His Word, praying and just being quiet so you can hear Him speak to you. Then, when life gets tough you know Him well enough to know He will take care of you because of His promises.

The Worry Queen

Thorns and weeds push in front of real plants so they can get water and food from the soil.

In this example, Jesus teaches that people who hear the message of God's love but still let worry and other things take over their hearts and minds are like those seeds that fell among thorns.

The truth of God's love gets pushed aside by the worries of life so they don't grow strong in their faith.

"Other seed fell among thorns, which grew up with it and choked the plants. The seed that fell among thorns stands for those who hear, but as they go on their way they are choked by life's worries, riches and pleasures, and they do not mature."

※ Luke 8:7, 14

Living It

If there is one thing Kathy is good at, it is worry. She worries about whether her friends really like her, her grades, how well she is doing in sports and music. She is a really good worrier.

That's not a good thing, because worry keeps her from trusting God. Her mind and heart are so busy worrying that they don't have time to learn about God and grow stronger in trusting Him.

Healthy Soil, Healthy Heart

"Still other seed fell on good soil. It came up and yielded a crop, a hundred times more than was sown. But the seed on good soil stands for those with a noble and good heart, who hear the Word, retain it, and by persevering produce a good crop."

Luke 8:8, 15

In the final part of Jesus' story about seeds, He said that some of the seed fell on good soil. It took root and grew into strong, healthy plants.

This part of Jesus' story is an example of people who hear the message of God's love and let it take root in their hearts, growing a strong faith within them. These are healthy Christians who serve God with obedient hearts.

Living It

Some girls fight everything they are taught. They argue and challenge everything. Lucy is like that. She questions everything.

When the message of God's love is shared with her, Lucy questions it. She reads through the Bible and learns how much God loves her. Lucy invites Jesus into her heart and lets His love take root and grow. She learns to love Him more and more.

Humble Hearts

Another way to read this verse is to replace "meek" with "humble." Jesus is saying that a humble person, one who puts others' needs in front of her own, will be blessed.

"Blessed are the meek, for they will inherit the earth."
Matthew 5:5

Jesus' lessons are always about love – for others and for God. A girl who is full of pride and concerned only about herself does not show God-based love and concern for others.

Living It

Hannah doesn't think about humility. She doesn't have to think about it, because it comes naturally to her. Oh, she doesn't put herself down or dismiss her own strengths and gifts.

Hannah has real concern for others. So, she thinks about what others need and how they feel. She puts others before herself and by doing that she shows God's love to them.

Living with Purpose

"The Spirit of the Lord is on Me, because He has anointed Me to proclaim good news to the poor. He has sent Me to proclaim freedom for the prisoners and recovery of sight for the blind, to set the oppressed free, to proclaim the year of the Lord's favor."

Luke 4:18-19

These words of Jesus are very important because He was actually quoting verses from the Old Testament prophet, Isaiah.

Why is that important? Because it shows once again that Jesus cared enough about Scripture to pay attention to it. Jesus shared that He is the person Isaiah was talking about.

God sent Jesus to earth with a specific mission. Accepting Jesus sets you free from many things. He gives freedom.

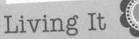

Living It

Jesus knew why He left heaven and came to earth. He knew that He had a job to do. Everything He did was for others. He taught others about God's wonderful love. He did whatever He could to help others.

Serving God and others is what Jesus is all about. What are you all about? What's your purpose today?

The Kingdom Is Near

God's goal is for every person to come to know Him in a personal way. The only way that can happen is for a girl to repent of her sins.

That means to be truly, honestly sorry for the bad things you do; even the things you can't help but do. Then you can ask God to help you stop doing those things and make every effort yourself to stop.

Believing the good news means believing the news that Jesus died for your sins, that He was raised back to life by God and wants to know you and help you.

> "The kingdom of God has come near. Repent and believe the good news!"
>
> Mark 1:15

Living It

Lorie has heard the "good news" and her parents are Christians who are very serious about their faith in Jesus. Lorie doesn't quite get the "kingdom of God is near"-thing. Does that mean her life on earth is going to be short? Not necessarily. It means that God is returning soon.

Therefore, it is important to be a child of God, to be certain in the knowledge that you will be with Him, should tomorrow be the day of His return. Repent and believe and become a part of His kingdom!

Few Words – Great Meaning

"When you pray, do not keep on babbling like pagans, for they think they will be heard because of their many words."

Matthew 6:7

In Jesus' day, some people prayed aloud just to show off. They used fancy words and just kept talking and talking and talking.

They thought it made them look super spiritual if they prayed fancy prayers. But, their prayers were not from the heart. They didn't really care about the things they prayed for or about the people around them. Their fancy prayers did not make God listen.

Living It

Nicole is very shy. The thought of praying aloud in front of other people makes her very nervous. She listens to some people pray and they use such big words and say things so beautifully. She doesn't feel she can do that. But the feelings in her heart are beautiful as she prays for others.

Guess what? It doesn't matter whether she can pray using fancy words, because God hears what is in her heart. Fancy prayers are fine if the person praying them truly means them. Even simple one-word prayers from the heart are heard by God.

Respect for God's House

Treat God's house with respect – that is Jesus' message here. Jesus was in the temple when He said this.

There were people in the temple selling animals to be offered as sacrifices. That was normal, except they were overcharging and cheating the people so they could make more money.

That made Jesus angry, because the temple should be a place where the people were safe and treated with respect. It was God's house, just as your church is today.

"Get these out of here! Stop turning My Father's house into a market!"
John 2:16

Living It

"Mom, can I take my school fundraiser order form to church and see if I can get a lot of orders?" Penny asked.

Her mom didn't think that was such a great idea. "You can contact our church friends to see if they would like to order things, but not at church. There is a time and a place for selling. Church is for worshiping God," Mom replied. Respecting God's house is important.

Number One

> "Give to the one who asks you, and do not turn away from the one who wants to borrow from you."
>
> Matthew 5:42

Jesus spoke these words as He was teaching about the folly of trying to get even with others.

Instead of trying to come out on top in every argument or fight, just back off. You don't have to always win. In fact, when someone, even someone who isn't a friend, wants to borrow something from you or asks you for something, give it to them. While you're at it, give them more than they ask for.

Living It

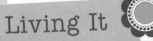

Audra is so mad at Melissa that she can't think about anything else. Melissa really hurt Audra's feelings. They haven't even spoken to each other for several weeks and Audra is just fine with that.

But then one afternoon, Melissa comes up and asks a favor ... just like nothing ever happened. What will Audra do? Tell Melissa, "no way!" or forgive and forget and move on? If she follows Jesus' teaching, what do you think she should do?

Real Rest

Jesus was always surrounded by large crowds of people who wanted to hear Him teach about God or see Him do miracles. It was hard for Jesus and His disciples to get any time alone.

Jesus' disciples had just told Him that they hadn't even had time to eat. Jesus cared about them just as He cares about you and He knows that one basic thing you need is to get away from the chaos of life and just be alone with Him for a while.

That will give you rest.

> "Come with Me by yourselves to a quiet place and get some rest."
> Mark 6:31

Living It

Kayla is in her school play. Rehearsals have been every night for three weeks. On top of that she has homework, chores at home, choir practice and church. She hardly ever has any downtime.

Kayla is tired and getting discouraged. She will feel better if she can just take a few minutes every day and be alone with Jesus. That will give her rest.

Promises Fulfilled

> "Do not think that I have come to abolish the Law or the Prophets; I have not come to abolish them but to fulfill them."
>
> Matthew 5:17

This is so cool. The Bible is 66 books divided into two sections – the Old Testament and the New Testament.

The Old Testament was written before Jesus ever came to earth, but it predicted His coming. Jesus recognized the Old Testament teachings and confirmed that He was the bridge between the Old and New Testaments.

Everything the Old Testament predicted was fulfilled by Jesus! Still today, both parts of the Bible are important.

Living It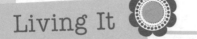

The Bible is a big book, isn't it? Some parts of it are hard to understand. So, do you just read the parts you understand? By reading the Old Testament you will see how God takes care of His people. You will learn how He saves His people so that His word continues through the years.

You will actually understand the whole Bible better as you see that the things that happened in the New Testament were predicted in the Old Testament. Jesus is the Savior who was promised hundreds of years before He came.

Special You

Jesus told this story to show how much God loves each and every person.

Every single person is important enough to God that He will search high and low to make sure everyone has a chance to know Him.

Jesus said God would leave the crowd to go and look for one follower who has wandered away.

"Suppose one of you has a hundred sheep and loses one of them. Doesn't he leave the ninety-nine in the open country and go after the lost sheep until he finds it?"

Luke 15:4

Living It

Olivia isn't anyone special. Well, at least she doesn't think she is. She's just an average girl of average intelligence and average talents. She looks around her and sees girls who are really special – everyone knows they are.

But what Olivia doesn't realize is that to God she is incredibly special, because He loves her. He feels the same way about you! God loves you more than you can possibly imagine!

Truly Serving God

"You will always have the poor among you, but you will not always have Me."

John 12:8

Does this seem like an odd statement for Jesus to make? After all, He is all about caring for others. Yes, He is and He often taught that people should take care of one another.

But, even knowing that, Jesus also taught that there is nothing more important than serving God. Love God. Honor God. Do not let anything or anyone become more important than Him.

If you focus on loving and serving God then you will do the right things in your life.

Living It

Lila and her family are super involved with working in the food pantry in their town. Lila loves working there and she is really good at making posters to advertise the need for donations to the pantry. Lila feels like she is doing something good by working there. It is a good thing, no doubt about that.

But Lila has allowed the food pantry to be so important to her that she doesn't think very often about God or serving Him. She works in the food pantry, but not as a way of serving God.

Work to Be Done

In the original Greek, this statement reads, "As you are going, make disciples ..." So Jesus assumed that His followers would continue the work He started, telling people about God's love and teaching about Him.

Jesus told His followers to baptize new believers because that identified them as Christians. The instructions He gave could have seemed overwhelming, but He reminded them that He was with them – always.

"Therefore go and make disciples of all nations, baptizing them in the name of the Father and of the Son and of the Holy Spirit, and teaching them to obey everything I have commanded you."
Matthew 28:19-20

Living It

These words were not just spoken to instruct the disciples who traveled with Jesus. They were also instructions for you and all believers.

Everyone has a responsibility to share the message of God's love and to teach new believers to know Him better so they can obey Him and live for Him. You never have to be afraid that you can't do the work, because Jesus is with you ... always.

True Authority!

"The Son of Man has authority on earth to forgive sins."

Mark 2:10

Religious leaders of the day constantly criticized Jesus. They looked for ways to trick Him and tried to prove that He was breaking the religious laws of the Old Testament.

But, of course, He hadn't. He answered their accusations with statements like this, proclaiming that He had the authority of God to forgive sins.

Living It

Many times the result of Jesus' forgiveness of sin also included a physical healing because He saw the faith of the people who came to Him.

Faith in Jesus and in the plan of salvation that He brings makes it possible for you to be with Him in heaven some day. All of this is possible only because Jesus has the authority to forgive sins. What a wonderful gift!

Who Needs a Doctor?

The ministry of Jesus focuses on sin – the bad, mean and hurtful things that people do. Things that are disobedient to the way Jesus wants people to live.

He wants to help sinners stop sinning – that is what He means by helping the sick. Righteous people do not think they need help. Sinners know they do.

> "It is not the healthy who need a doctor, but the sick. But go and learn what this means: 'I desire mercy, not sacrifice.' For I have not come to call the righteous, but sinners."
> Matthew 9:12-13

Living It

People who think they never sin are full of pride (which, by the way, is a sin). They think they are so perfect that they do not need Jesus at all. It's very hard to help someone like that.

Patty is like that. She says she doesn't do anything wrong. So, she doesn't pay any attention to Jesus. But, Jesus pays attention to her. She is "sick" and she needs Him more than anyone!

Jesus' Love in Action

> "If you lend to those from whom you expect repayment, what credit is that to you? Even sinners lend to sinners, expecting to be repaid in full."
>
> Luke 6:34

Once again, Jesus drives home the point that treating others as you would like to be treated is very important.

If a person treats only her friends with respect or generosity, so what? Anyone can do that. But if you unselfishly reach out to those with whom you do not have a relationship and show mercy to them, that is God's love in action.

Mercy helps others and expects nothing in return. It is a different kind of love than the love shown by those who do not know Christ.

Living It

"I don't get you," Cathy said. "Why do you hang out with Kyrah? She's not part of our group." Carol knew that Cathy didn't get it but she answered, "She needs help with math and I can help her." "Yeah, but what's in it for you?" Cathy asked.

Yep, she didn't get it. Sometimes helping others in any way you can is just the right thing to do; especially girls who aren't a part of your group. It's Jesus' love in action.

Secret Giving

The Christian life is not about showing off. Jesus said that if you do good deeds just to show off or to get praise from other people, then you've missed the point.

Helping others, being generous, sacrificing for someone else – those are all important things. But, if you live that way just so people will say, "Wow, what a kind and generous person," then that's all the reward you'll get.

Do things anonymously so that only you and God know about your generosity.

"Your Father, who sees what is done in secret, will reward you."
Matthew 6:4

Living It

Macy and her family have a cool tradition. Every so often they make up a box of goodies: non-perishable food items, warm mittens, books, toys for small children. They secretly leave it on the front porch of a family which is struggling financially.

Maybe the parents have lost their jobs or perhaps a family member has been sick. It's a nice treat and help for the family. Macy and her family get so much joy from doing it. Even though no one except them (and God) knows they were the givers.

July

The Kingdom of God

"Very truly I tell you, no one can enter the kingdom of God unless they are born of water and the Spirit."

John 3:5

One time a religious leader came to Jesus and asked about the miracles He did.

Most of the religious leaders – the Pharisees – didn't understand the spiritual side of Jesus' teaching because they lived by laws. So, when Jesus said that a person had to be born of the Spirit, it made no sense to them.

When you ask Jesus into your heart the Holy Spirit comes in and lives there, leading, guiding and loving. That makes you a part of God's kingdom.

Living It

This teaching by Jesus is important because it proves that just doing good things or being a nice person is not enough to bring a girl into the kingdom of God.

It's wonderful to be nice and do good things, but the Spirit cleans your heart from sin and makes you a new person on the inside. Welcome to God's kingdom!

Revealing Light

Jesus is the Light of the world. When His light shines on your heart then you (and others) can see you for who you are. Any selfishness, hatred, dishonesty, laziness ... whatever is there is shown.

Some people respond to that by asking Jesus to clean up their lives. Some say, "Hey, I like the way I am." Those are the ones Jesus is talking about here. They like the darkness instead of the light because they like doing evil things. Too bad.

"This is the verdict: Light has come into the world, but people loved darkness instead of light because their deeds were evil."
John 3:19

Living It

Annie thinks she is a pretty nice girl. After all, she has never stolen anything or hurt anyone badly. She doesn't have any of the bad habits other girls have. She's good.

But, when her heart is opened to hear Jesus' words, His light helps her see that she is jealous of her best friend, she is mean to her little brother, she sometimes tells half-truths to her mom. Yeah, there is stuff in her heart that she needs Jesus to clean up. Annie doesn't love darkness so she asks Him to help.

Light Changes Things

> "Whoever lives by the truth comes into the light, so that it may be seen plainly that what they have done has been done in the sight of God."
>
> John 3:21

If a person lives by the truth, then she has nothing to hide. So she is willing to step into the light and allow all things to be revealed – the good and the bad.

She is willing to let all see that who she is and the changes in her heart and life are due to Christ and His power and love.

Her good deeds are because of Him and the improvements in her thoughts and actions are, too.

Living It

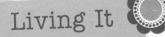

When Sandy asked Jesus to be her Savior, He showed her some things in her heart that needed to be changed. One of those was the way she treated her mother and father.

She was rebellious toward them and argued about everything. They do not know Jesus and now Sandy has a chance to be a witness to them. So she went to them and said "Mom, Dad, I asked Jesus into my heart and He showed me that I've not treated you very well. I just want you to know that I'm sorry and with His help, I will do better."

Sold Out for God

Jesus left no room for compromise with this command. Love God completely. Love God totally. Give Him your heart – your emotions. Give Him your soul – your being. Give Him your mind – your thoughts.

God will not share first place in your heart, soul and mind with anything else. He is to be Number One. You will never be sorry.

> "'Love the Lord your God with all your heart and with all your soul and with all your mind.' This is the first and greatest commandment."
>
> Matthew 22:37-38

Living It

Mallory has heard this verse like a bazillion times. She knows that God must be above all other things in her heart, soul and mind. But she doesn't see that in her own heart something keeps knocking Him out of first place – her friends.

She cares very much about what they think of her and how she is fitting in with them that sometimes they are more important than God. Yikes. Time to fix that, right? First place in her heart, soul and mind belongs to God alone!

Second Commandment

"The second [commandment] is like it: 'Love your neighbor as yourself.' All the Law and the Prophets hang on these two commandments."

Matthew 22:39-40

Love, love, love. Jesus had just taught His followers that loving God with all their heart, soul and mind was the greatest commandment. Now, He says the second greatest commandment is to love others.

Basic stuff – and these two commands are basic to everything else He teaches. Absolutely everything. This totally blasted the Pharisees' teachings that living for God meant obeying lots of rules, especially if those rules showed no love to God or others.

Love is what it's all about.

Living It

It's so tempting to judge other people for what they say and do. Maya knows that. She totally dropped one friend because of the way that girl treated her. Maya knows that this friend is from a messy family situation and she doesn't know Jesus.

What Maya learns from this command of Jesus is that she must love this friend. Love, love, love. Love in a way that doesn't expect anything in return. Look beyond the unkind words or actions and see what might be causing them. Just love.

Source of Peace

Life is stressful. At times problems can be overwhelming. There are people who attack you for who you are, what you believe and how you live.

Sometimes people criticize you simply because you are a Jesus-follower. He knows that and encourages you to stick close to Him. He gives real peace, not the kind of peace that comes from agreeing with other people, but real peace that settles deep in your soul.

> "Peace I leave with you; My peace I give you. I do not give to you as the world gives. Do not let your hearts be troubled and do not be afraid."
>
> John 14:27

Living It

Peace is not something Darcy is familiar with. There isn't much of it in her family. They seem to go from one crisis to another. It's hard for Darcy to know peace when her parents are stressed about money or a sick parent or some other problem.

Her friends cannot really help so where does Darcy find peace? Jesus. She can tell Him anything that is weighing on her heart. He cares. And He promises to take care of her and her family.

Powerful Protection

> "My prayer is not that You take them out of the world but that You protect them from the evil one."
>
> John 17:15

Jesus knows that Satan goes after people who want to obey Jesus. He will do everything in his power to stop that obedience. He will make them question God's love for them. He will try to convince them that they're not good enough for God to love.

Jesus knew that would happen, so why didn't He ask God to take Christians out of the world? Because Christians have work to do here – telling others about God's love. Jesus didn't ask God to take Christians to heaven, but He did ask for protection from Satan for them.

Living It

Lindsey wonders how many times a day this prayer is answered in her life. How often does God protect her from some attack of Satan?

She knows that sometimes negative thoughts about herself pop into her mind. Thoughts about how she isn't any good at things, but just as quickly some kind of encouragement comes along. That has to be God protecting her. Lindsey is so thankful for God's protection and He is more powerful than Satan!

Jesus' Broken Heart

Jesus took His disciples with Him to the Garden of Gethsemane on the night He was arrested. He knew what was coming – betrayal, arrest, torture, death.

Why was His soul overwhelmed with such sorrow? Because of the pain that was ahead for Him? Maybe. But He probably felt sorrow, too, that the people who heard Him teach and knew of His miracles had still rejected Him and the message of God's love.

That broke His heart.

> "My soul is overwhelmed with sorrow to the point of death. Stay here and keep watch with Me."
> Matthew 26:38

Living It

Maria loves God. She gave her heart to Him when she was only six years old. Ever since then she has loved reading her Bible, praying and sharing God's love with her family and friends.

Maria often asks God to break her heart with what breaks His so that she will know the urgency and importance of sharing His love with others.

Real Prayer Power

> "Everyone who asks receives; the one who seeks finds; and to the one who knocks, the door will be opened."
>
> Matthew 7:8

Jesus wants you to take prayer seriously because prayer makes a difference. That's why He made the point of telling you that asking, seeking and knocking brings results.

Keep your heart focused on God so that the things you ask, seek and knock for are aligned with His will and are not selfish or self-centered.

Living It

Sometimes Kelly's prayers are just a long list of "I want this" or "Do that for me." After all, she figures that Jesus said to ask for whatever she wants. Yeah, well Kelly doesn't really understand Jesus' instructions.

She needs to remember the full picture of wanting God's will to be done and desiring to serve Him with her whole heart. Jesus often says to be focused on loving God and others. Love – that's what should guide her prayers.

Bright Lights

Jesus is the Light of the world and in the verse just before this one He says that those who believe in Him are also lights in the world.

Jesus knows that life as a Christian is not easy. You may not always be treated kindly by those who do not share your beliefs. However, He doesn't let Christians off the hook. He doesn't say, "Well, don't worry about things. Just keep quiet about your faith." Nope, He says to let your light shine – do not hide it.

Your light is **His** light and it will light the way for many people!

> "Neither do people light a lamp and put it under a bowl. Instead they put it on its stand, and it gives light to everyone in the house."
>
> Matthew 5:15

Living It

Delia is a new Christian so she is excited about her faith and wants to tell others about Jesus. However, some of her friends don't want to hear it and they get pretty rude toward her.

Delia could just be quiet and go on with her life, but she doesn't. She keeps sharing her faith, kindly and with respect. She is Jesus' light to her friends!

Honoring God's Word

> "Truly I tell you, until heaven and earth disappear, not the smallest letter, not the least stroke of a pen, will by any means disappear from the Law until everything is accomplished."
>
> Matthew 5:18

Jesus respects the Scriptures. Even though He had knowledge of Scripture from God's viewpoint, He always communicated to those around Him how important Scripture is.

In this verse He emphasizes the total truth of Scripture and that not one word of it will change until everything it teaches happens. A pretty good reason to study Scripture, eh?

Living It

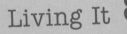

Jennie has just got her own cell phone. She spends lots of time texting with her friends. She quickly learned the text lingo abbreviations that make texting faster. She spends so much time on her phone that her mom has threatened to take it away.

There isn't much that's more important to her than her phone ... not even the Bible. Jennie is a Christian, but she doesn't read or try to understand her Bible. She really doesn't get how important Scripture is.

Obeying No Matter What

Jesus was very clear about honoring Scripture. God doesn't take disobedience lightly.

He urges, encourages and expects His children to know and obey Scripture. It makes life better – better relationships with others, honor toward God, self-respect and care for yourself. It makes sense.

Those who honor Scripture will be honored in heaven. Those who do not and encourage others to also disobey will answer for that in heaven.

> "Anyone who sets aside one of the least of these commands and teaches others accordingly will be called least in the kingdom of heaven, but whoever practices and teaches these commands will be called great in the kingdom of heaven."
>
> Matthew 5:19

Living It

"Katie, do me a favor?" Tessa whispered. "Just slide your test paper over a bit and let me see your answers. I'm so bad at math and you're so good. Please, pretty please?"

Katie was tempted. She knew that Tessa and math did not connect at all and Tessa was a good friend. But she replied, "Tessa, I can't do that. The Bible teaches that cheating is wrong. I'd be happy to help you study next time, though, OK?" Katie is honoring Scripture and encouraging Tessa to do the same.

Making Peace

> "Settle matters quickly with your adversary who is taking you to court. Do it while you are still together on the way, or your adversary may hand you over to the judge, and the judge may hand you over to the officer, and you may be thrown into prison."
>
> Matthew 5:25

Jesus encourages healthy relationships with the people around you.

So, if someone claims that you have wronged her – settle the problem. Take the lead and talk with her to set things right.

What happens when you ignore problems? They can grow into bigger and bigger problems which will take a lot more time and energy to solve.

Living It

Connie and Terra are fighting. Terra is angry that Connie blabbed Terra's secrets to all their friends. Connie knows what Jesus says about settling problems so she asks if she can talk to Terra.

Connie admits that she did something wrong and asks Terra to forgive her. The matter is settled privately and while it may take Terra a while to trust Connie again, they are working on it!

Total Forgiveness

This is hard, isn't it? Forgiving someone who has hurt you is a difficult thing to do.

You might feel more like getting even with them. Or maybe you just decide to ignore the person and even feel pretty noble about that; like it might be the Christian thing to do. Actually, the Christian thing to do is to forgive the person who hurts you. Totally, completely forgive her.

After all, God forgives you when you hurt others or Him. He forgives you over and over and over.

> "If you do not forgive others their sins, your Father will not forgive your sins."
> Matthew 6:15

Living It

Brooke and Alison used to be best friends. They were besties for about six years. Then suddenly Alison dumped Brooke.

There was no reason that Brooke knew of but it hurt and she wanted to get even. After a while she decided that wasn't a good way to feel. Instead she just pretended Alison didn't exist. She even thought that was a good way to feel – after all, she didn't hate Alison. But, as Brooke reads Scripture, she understands that "not hating" is not enough. She needs to forgive, completely forgive, especially if she expects God to forgive her!

A Heavenly Reward

"When you fast, do not look somber as the hypocrites do, for they disfigure their faces to show others they are fasting. Truly I tell you, they have received their reward in full."

Matthew 6:16

Don't do things for show. When you fast or pray or serve or do anything that is supposed to be for God then don't draw attention to yourself.

Don't try to look like you are starving when you are fasting. Don't try to get people to feel sorry for you or try to make people think you are awesomely spiritual. If you do that, don't expect God to bless you or what you are offering Him. Your only reward is whatever people say about you.

Living It

You may know girls who need a lot of attention. Girls who want others to notice if they are hurt or sick. Girls who want praise when they sing well or play well in sports or anything else. Girls who want a pat on the back for any good thing they do. Even when they are doing something good for other people, they want everyone to know it.

Girls like this have missed the point of serving God. They are looking for praise from people, not from God.

Between God and You

Some things should just be between you and God – no one else.

Fasting is a time when you don't eat, but spend time in prayer and focus on God. It is no one else's business that you are fasting.

If you are concerned about what others think, then you aren't really focused on God, are you?

"When you fast, put oil on your head and wash your face, so that it will not be obvious to others that you are fasting, but only to your Father, who is unseen; and your Father, who sees what is done in secret, will reward you."

Matthew 6:17-18

Living It

What does it mean to be focused on God? Well, you know what it's like to be focused on something you enjoy a lot – music, sports, books, friends, crafts – right? You think about that thing a lot and you want to be doing it all the time.

Being focused on God is like that – thinking about Him, reading His Word, praying, trying to understand what He wants for you. This is not stuff for other people to be involved in. It is between you and God.

No Worries

> "Can any one of you by worrying add a single hour to your life?"
> Matthew 6:27

Jesus knows that worry can suck energy right out of your life.

Worry takes away hope. It destroys joy. Worry means you don't believe God. Trust and worry can't live in the same heart.

If you truly believe that Jesus loves you and that His Word is true, then what do you have to worry about?

Living It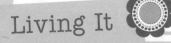

"Not worry? Are you crazy? How can I not worry?" Mara thought. "I don't care what Jesus said. He didn't know what was going to happen to my family. He probably expects me to worry."

No, Mara, He doesn't. Jesus is not surprised by anything that happens to you. He can take care of you and handle any problem that comes up.

So, save your energy. Let Jesus take care of things.

What Do You Need?

The thing about worry is that most people worry about things they have no control over. God knows what your needs are even before you know what they are.

Just before this Jesus pointed out how God takes care of the flowers in the field. He makes them grow and watches over them.

God loves you even more than He loves flowers. So trust Him!

"Do not worry, saying, 'What shall we eat?' or 'What shall we drink?' or 'What shall we wear?' For the pagans run after all these things, and your heavenly Father knows that you need them."

Matthew 6:31-32

Living It

Tami cares about impressing people. So, she is super concerned about wearing the "right" designer labels. It matters to her to be seen in the "right" restaurants. She wants people to think she is super cool. It matters so much to her that she worries about it.

Tami isn't worrying about what she "needs," she is worrying about what she "wants". Tami needs an attitude adjustment to just be concerned about what she needs and to know that God will take care of those needs.

Seek First His Kingdom

> "Seek first His kingdom and His righteousness, and all these things will be given to you as well."
>
> Matthew 6:33

Keep your eyes on what is important. Some people worry about everyday things like food or clothes. Some worry about money and success. Some worry about what other people think of them.

Jesus said not to worry about any of that stuff. He said to keep your eyes on the goal of knowing and serving God and not to worry about any of the other stuff.

Jesus will take care of everything you need.

Living It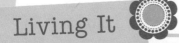

Jennie worries a lot about what her friends think of her. She tries to fit in by liking what they like, wearing what they wear, liking people they like. Her focus is on pleasing them, not God.

Jennie has lost sight of what is really important. If she would focus on knowing and serving God, then He will supply her needs ... including good friends.

Eye Dangers

Jesus is all about relationships and fairness and treating others well.

So this command is to not criticize your friends and family members for the small things they do. Instead, look at the things you do that hurt others. You will probably find that your actions are worse than others'.

Once you correct your own actions you will be able to more clearly see how to help others.

"You hypocrite, first take the plank out of your own eye, and then you will see clearly to remove the speck from your brother's eye."
Matthew 7:5

Living It

"Olivia is such a loser," Kyra thought. "She always has to be the center of attention. When she is in the room no one pays any attention to anyone else. It makes me crazy. Life is not always all about her!"

Kyra may be right about Olivia, but she hasn't yet admitted to herself that she is jealous of Olivia because she wants attention herself! Take care of your own weaknesses before you criticize another, Kyra. You just might understand her better.

Protect the Sacred

"Do not give dogs what is sacred; do not throw your pearls to pigs. If you do, they may trample them under their feet, and turn and tear you to pieces."

Matthew 7:6

What is the most valuable thing you have to give to another person? Your heart and loyalty, right?

Yeah, so Jesus said to be careful where you place your heart and loyalty. If you give it to someone who isn't worthy of it, they won't respect your loyalty. They will trample it and totally wreck it. They will not have any concern for you or what's best for you.

Give sacred things (like your heart) to the One who deserves it – God.

Living It

Danielle is sort of the boss of all the girls in her class. They all do what she says even though they don't really like her. They are more afraid of her. Rachel is afraid of her, too. In fact, she is so afraid that she does whatever Danielle says. She gives all her loyalty to Danielle, because she is afraid if she doesn't she won't have any friends.

But, Danielle doesn't care about Rachel at all. She only cares about herself. So, she takes Rachel's loyalty and devotion and throws it away. She doesn't care at all.

God's Wonderful Gifts

God loves you more than you can possibly imagine. Jesus wants you to understand that.

As much as your parents love you and give you wonderful gifts, God loves you more and wants to give you everything you need and even things you don't need – blessings beyond anything you can ask for or dream of.

> "Which of you, if your son asks for bread, will give him a stone? Or if he asks for a fish, will give him a snake? If you, then, though you are evil, know how to give good gifts to your children, how much more will your Father in heaven give good gifts to those who ask Him!"
> Matthew 7:9-11

Living It

Claire reads this verse and sometimes wonders what it means. After all, she doesn't have **everything** she wants. And, as she looks around at her friends she sees she doesn't have all the stuff they have.

Claire doesn't quite get the meaning of God's gifts. His gifts aren't "stuff," they are love, joy, hope, help, protection, the promise of heaven. Sometimes His gifts are beautiful flowers, rainbows or the smile from a loved one that just reminds you that God is with you, loving you more than you know.

The Jesus Way

> "In everything, do to others what you would have them do to you, for this sums up the Law and the Prophets."
>
> Matthew 7:12

Jesus teaches His followers to treat other people well. He knows that it's easy to get caught up in selfish attitudes and think only about how things affect you. When that happens, you start treating other people badly. Don't do that.

Treat others the way you want them to treat you – then even if they aren't nice back, your conscience is clear. And they just might begin to treat you better!

Living It

Mallory and Jenna are both gymnasts. They are both pretty good but Mallory is just a bit better and usually wins first place in the meets. Jenna is jealous so she treats Mallory poorly. Then she starts spreading untrue rumors about Mallory. It gets ugly.

Mallory's response, however, is not to be mean back. Instead, she is consistently kind to Jenna. She treats Jenna the way she would like to be treated. After a while, Jenna apologizes to Mallory and begins treating her as a friend again. That's the Jesus way.

The Path to Life

Jesus knows that the road to life with Him, the road to heaven, is not always going to be the popular way.

People who aren't interested in knowing Jesus travel together down a wide road that doesn't lead to life with Him. It's comfortable because you are with a crowd, but it's a crowd going nowhere.

Pay attention to Jesus and to God's Word and find the narrow road that leads to life with Him.

> "Small is the gate and narrow the road that leads to life, and only a few find it."
> Matthew 7:14

Living It

Lucy has one or two friends from church, but they aren't the popular crowd by any means. So, when a group of girls accept her as their friend, she's thrilled! The thing is, to be with them she has to think the way they think, act the way they act and treat others the way they do. These girls aren't always nice and have no interest in knowing God. Yes, Lucy is with a crowd, but they are going nowhere. Lucy decides it's more important to know and obey Jesus. She chooses the narrow road that leads to life with Him and she is much happier because of it.

Good Fruit/Bad Fruit

"Every good tree bears good fruit, but a bad tree bears bad fruit. A good tree cannot bear bad fruit, and a bad tree cannot bear good fruit."

Matthew 7:17-18

Jesus uses the illustration of trees and fruit a lot. He makes it an example of a Jesus-follower's life.

It is basic. A healthy tree has good fruit, but an unhealthy tree has bad fruit. A person who has Jesus in her heart should have good fruit – love and honor for God and love for others. A person who doesn't have Jesus in her heart will not have good fruit.

Living It

It's true that people who do not know Jesus can be kind and loving. But, there is a depth to a Christian's love that makes her unselfish and very giving. It's "good fruit" that comes from Jesus' love.

Andie is like that. She encourages others to succeed and be in the spotlight in front of her. She gives time and energy to tutor little kids. She plays with her neighbor's little kids so the mom can do chores when she would rather be hanging out with her friends. Good fruit like that comes from Jesus.

Truth Fruit

There were people in Jesus' day (as there are today) who talk a good deal about knowing God. They announce how they trust "the Big Guy upstairs" or call for prayer during a crisis.

> "By their fruit you will recognize them."
> Matthew 7:20

But these people may not know God at all. How do you know? Look at the "fruit" of their lives. If they treat others with respect and love and have a consistent relationship with God that shows good fruit, then yes, they probably know Jesus.

If they only acknowledge Jesus in a crisis or a big victory, then maybe not.

Living It

Miranda is a good runner and every time she wins a race she thrusts her arm in the air and thanks the "Big Guy" for helping her win.

Is Miranda a true Christian? While that is only for God to judge, the evidence in her life of care and compassion for others, kindness and helpfulness shows the truth. Also, her devotion to God by reading His Word and praying shows that God is a daily presence in her life. The fruit in her life shows the truth.

The Real Thing

"Many will say to Me on that day, 'Lord, Lord, did we not prophesy in Your name and in Your name drive out demons and in Your name perform many miracles?'
Then I will tell them plainly, 'I never knew you. Away from Me, you evildoers!'"
Matthew 7:22-23

Choosing to follow Jesus is a serious decision. Choosing **not** to follow Jesus is even more serious.

Jesus makes it very clear in these verses that fakers don't fool Him. People who claim to do God's work, but have not accepted Jesus as Savior are fakers. They may fool others, but when it comes to entering heaven they will find they haven't fooled Him. If they don't know Jesus, they won't enter heaven.

Living It

Debbie goes to church. She knows Bible verses; goes on mission trips; is part of a creative arts ministry team. She does Christian things and by outward appearance is a wonderful Christian.

But, she hasn't asked Jesus into her heart. She hasn't confessed her sins to Him. She likes doing Christian stuff, but she doesn't know the Savior. So, on the day when she wants to enter heaven, she will be turned away. It's not too late for Debbie, though. She can still ask Jesus to be her Savior!

A Firm Foundation

Following Jesus' teachings gives peace and purpose to life because you know you can trust Him. It's a firm foundation.

In the tough times of life, those who don't trust Jesus find that they have no foundation. If you've ever stood on a beach you know what it feels like when the water comes up over your feet and pulls the sand away. Like a house built on sand, when a storm comes the rain pulls the sand away and the house crashes down.

If your foundation is not firm (on God) then it will be pulled away in the storms of life.

> "Everyone who hears these words of Mine and does not put them into practice is like a foolish man who built his house on sand. The rain came down, the streams rose, and the winds blew and beat against that house, and it fell with a great crash."
>
> Matthew 7:26-27

Living It

Kim found out what the term "firm foundation" means. When her dad lost his job, Kim was scared. She was worried about her parents because they began fighting a lot.

Kim missed her friends when they had to move. But, she trusted God. She discovered that her firm foundation of Jesus' love carried her through the hard times.

Job Openings!

> "The harvest is plentiful but the workers are few. Ask the Lord of the harvest, therefore, to send out workers into His harvest field."
>
> Matthew 9:37-38

Jesus is focused on the reason He left heaven to come to earth – so people could know God personally.

When Jesus came to earth, He knew there were many people who didn't yet know God; many people who had not accepted Jesus as Savior. Jesus wants every person to have an opportunity to hear about God's love – every person for all time. So, He needs workers – you, for example. Jesus calls for workers and for His people to ask God to send more and more workers.

Living It

When Isabelle reads this verse it challenges her to do something. Isabelle has friends and family members who do not know Jesus. She prays for them to come to know Him, but what else can she do? Isabelle looks for chances to gently share her faith in Jesus and tell her friends and family members how much He means to her. She prays for people in other countries who have never had a chance to hear about Him and she thanks God for missionaries who dedicate their lives to go to those places and share the good news.

A Full Life

This is kind of a confusing statement, isn't it? Focus on the words about whoever loses their life will find it.

Losing your life – giving it over to Jesus – doesn't actually take it away. No, it enriches your life and gives you purpose, peace and joy.

So, actually, your life is found and it's better than before.

> "Whoever finds their life will lose it, and whoever loses their life for My sake will find it."
> Matthew 10:39

Living It

Nancy has always had a dream for her life. As long as she can remember she has wanted to be an artist when she grows up. She has planned for it and dreamt about it.

But, when Nancy accepted Jesus as her Savior her life took a new direction. Would that change her dream to be an artist? Nope, it just made it more focused. Now her art would be a way to glorify and honor Jesus. She didn't lose anything. She found a lot!

Humble Children

> "I praise You, Father, Lord of heaven and earth, because You have hidden these things from the wise and learned, and revealed them to little children."
>
> Matthew 11:25

The religious leaders of Jesus' day thought they knew everything. They thought they had all the answers about God and living for Him. But Jesus knew they didn't.

Jesus knew that the simple faith of a child was more pleasing to God than the arrogant religious leaders. Because of that, God lets those who have faith like little children understand more than those who think they have all the answers.

Living It

Cathy is kind of shy. She feels like she doesn't understand a lot about the Bible or living for God so she never says much about her faith. She knows some older girls who think they have it all figured out. They're always saying things like, "God told me this ... " or "The Bible says ... "

The truth is, however, they don't have everything figured out. They are kind of making up their own version of Christianity. Humble girls like Cathy understand a lot more than the arrogant girls. God opens their minds and hearts so they can understand.

August

Rules ... or Mercy?

"If any of you has a sheep and it falls into a pit on the Sabbath, will you not take hold of it and lift it out? How much more valuable is a person than a sheep! Therefore it is lawful to do good on the Sabbath."

Matthew 12:11-12

Mercy is at the heart of Jesus' message. Some people said that the only way to follow God was to live by a bunch of rules. Jesus didn't agree with that.

He taught that it shows more of God's love to take care of people whenever they need something – even if it seems to break a law of God.

Mercy and caring for others shows God's love.

Living It

The Pharisees of Jesus' time loved to live by rules. They had a long list of rules that they insisted everyone had to obey. Some of the rules were in the Bible. Some were not.

What they missed was that some rules – like no work on the Sabbath – just didn't make sense if someone was in danger and needed help. Aren't you glad that Jesus feels people are more important than rules?

Watch Your Words

What you say reflects what is in your heart. Jesus points this out very clearly.

That's why He notices every word you speak and why you will have to give a reason for everything you say. That includes things you say because you think they're funny or because you're angry or tired.

"I tell you that everyone will have to give account on the Day of Judgment for every empty word they have spoken."
Matthew 12:36

Living It

Vicki loves to make others laugh. She likes that she is known as the funny one in her crowd. That's OK, except sometimes her jokes are at the expense of someone else. She makes friends laugh by commenting on another girl's clothes. Sometimes she even makes insensitive remarks because it amuses someone.

After reading these words of Jesus she knows that the words she thought didn't hurt anyone, do hurt someone ... her! She will have to answer for them.

Eyes that See

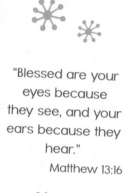

"Blessed are your eyes because they see, and your ears because they hear."

Matthew 13:16

Jesus had just finished talking about people who think they have all the answers.

People like that are so full of pride that they can't hear what anyone else says. They can't see how arrogant they are. They are so blinded that they can't even see the love of God around them.

They are blind and deaf to everything except themselves and their rules.

Living It

Lisa just accepted Christ a few weeks ago and is excited about everything she is learning about living for God. Lisa always thought that the Christian life was all about following a long list of rules and not having any fun at all. That was her experience with Christianity.

But, as Lisa reads her Bible and talks with other Christians, her eyes are opened to the unbelievable love of Christ and that's what she sees in every way He lived His life! That's what Lisa wants to show in her life, too – love for God and love for others.

The Growing Kingdom

Sometimes it seems as though the bad guys are winning. Bad news and terrible crimes fill the news. Evil people seem to get more powerful and richer.

But in the middle of all that bad stuff is God's kingdom: quietly working its way into the hearts of people and spreading through all the world.

Don't worry about the bad guys winning because just like yeast that silently makes bread rise, God's kingdom will be victorious over evil one day.

> "The kingdom of heaven is like yeast that a woman took and mixed into about sixty pounds of flour until it worked all through the dough."
>
> Matthew 13:33

Living It

Sometimes Ella gets scared just from hearing the TV news reports. Bad things happen right in the town where she lives. People do mean things to each other. Kids get hurt and people are killed. The news from around the world is even worse.

But Ella's mom reminds her that God is working, even in all the scary stuff. Every day more people accept Jesus and their hearts are changed to kindness and love. Ella and Mom pray every day for God's kingdom to keep growing so more and more people may know Him.

Growing Good Stuff

> "No," Jesus answered, "because while you are pulling the weeds, you may uproot the wheat with them. Let both grow together until the harvest. At that time I will tell the harvesters: First collect the weeds and tie them in bundles to be burned; then gather the wheat and bring it into My barn."
>
> Matthew 13:29-30

Jesus knows that some people will choose to accept Him as Savior and follow Him. Those people are the "wheat" in this verse. People who deny that He is the Savior and choose not to accept Him are the "weeds."

Both groups live together on earth, but when the Day of Judgment comes the "weed" people will not enter heaven. By their own choice they have denied Jesus and will not spend forever with Him.

Living It

This statement from Jesus really touches Susie's heart. She has accepted Jesus and is sure that she will someday be in heaven with Him.

However, Susie's mom, dad and brother do not know Him. The idea that she will not be with them in eternity makes her sad. Susie prays every day for her family. She looks for opportunities to share her faith with them and to show them Jesus' love by the way she treats them.

Basic Needs

Some people would have you believe that Jesus only cares about your soul – you know, spiritual things. But these words show that this isn't true.

Jesus cares about your whole life – even something so basic as whether or not you are hungry. How can you concentrate on listening to Jesus or growing in your faith if you are really, truly hungry?

Jesus wants to meet your basic needs.

> "I have compassion for these people; they have already been with Me three days and have nothing to eat. I do not want to send them away hungry, or they may collapse on the way."
> Matthew 15:32

Living It

Melanie wonders how these words can be true since there are some places in the world where people don't have enough food and water. Good question, Melanie. The thing is, God's people have a responsibility to take care of some aspects of God's work. There are many organizations that do their best to supply food to hungry people around the world.

But they need money and workers to do so. So, while God can certainly provide food in miraculous ways, He also expects His people to do their part to help others around the world.

Believing in Jesus' Plan

> "Get behind Me, Satan! You are a stumbling block to Me; you do not have in mind the concerns of God, but merely human concerns."
> Matthew 16:23

Wow, these are powerful words. Especially when you consider that Jesus said them to His friend, Peter.

Jesus had just predicted His own death, part of the reason for His coming to earth. Peter says, "No way! That won't happen." But Jesus knew His purpose for coming to earth and He followed that purpose.

Jesus couldn't let anyone stand in the way – not Peter, not you, not anyone!

Living It

Have you ever thought about how you would have responded if you lived at the time Jesus was on earth and heard Him say that He was going to die soon? Would you have said the same thing Peter did? Or would you have humbly thanked Jesus for sacrificing His own life? Well, how do you respond to Jesus' sacrifice now? Your words and actions show whether you are truly grateful. If you take Jesus' death lightly and disrespect Him, then He may say these same words to you. Have the things of God in your mind – His plan for all people to come to know Him.

Follow Jesus

Jesus had just told His disciples that He was going to die. That must have been a scary thing for them to hear. They may have wondered if their lives were in danger, too, since they were close followers of His.

Jesus wanted His followers to put aside any fear of suffering or pain. That is important for you, too. Focus on God's plan and how you can be a part of it and follow Him, no matter what.

> "Whoever wants to be My disciple must deny themselves and take up their cross and follow Me."
> Matthew 16:24

Living It

Nora is a Christian, but she is at a crossroads. One of her teachers does not believe in God and openly makes fun of anyone who does. As Nora listens to him rant and rave about how ridiculous Christianity is, she knows that she can just be quiet and let it happen.

Or, she can respectfully tell him that she disagrees and that God is a very real presence in her life. Scary, but that's what denying self and taking up her cross to follow Jesus means.

What's Most Important?

> "What good will it be for someone to gain the whole world, yet forfeit their soul? Or what can anyone give in exchange for their soul?"
>
> Matthew 16:26

Some people have big dreams of what they want to accomplish in life. Many dream of being rich beyond belief. Some dream of fame and recognition. Others want to be at the top of their chosen careers.

These are all fine dreams but, according to Jesus, if you accomplish any of these things but don't take care of your soul by accepting Him and living for Him, what good is any of it?

Deal with the really important thing first – your relationship with God.

Living It

Olivia has big dreams. She plays the violin and practices for hours every day. Olivia dreams of being first chair in the high school orchestra, going on to college and then becoming first chair in a big symphony orchestra. Olivia dreams that someday people will say she is the best violinist ever!

However, all of Olivia's dreams are focused on herself. She does not think about accepting Jesus, even though she has heard about His love for her. Olivia may become the best violinist in the world, but that won't get her into heaven. Only accepting Jesus will.

Make Changes Now

Jesus promised His followers that one day He will come back to earth and take His followers to heaven with Him. That will be an amazing day!

It will also be a day of coming face to face with how you have lived your life. Jesus will reward you for your obedience to Him. There will be no hiding or justifying any of the times you were disobedient and no way to change any of it.

Changes in how you live can only be made now.

> "The Son of Man is going to come in His Father's glory with His angels, and then He will reward each person according to what they have done."
>
> Matthew 16:27

Living It

Sandy is full of pride. Seriously, she feels she is the best at everything and wants everyone to know that. Sandy is all about Sandy. However, reading this verse made her stop and think that someday she will answer to God for the way she behaves.

God is not a fan of pride. He wouldn't like how she treats others. Sandy decides to do something about her behavior. She begins praying each day for God to take her pride away and fill her with humility and love.

Powerful Faith

"If you have faith as small as a mustard seed, you can say to this mountain, 'Move from here to there,' and it will move. Nothing will be impossible for you."

Matthew 17:20

As humans, we tend to believe in what we can see. Things that must be taken simply by faith are harder for us. But because God's kingdom is a spiritual kingdom, much of it must be taken by faith.

Jesus encourages that faith by telling us that we can do amazing things if we just have faith. Think about the miracles Jesus did when He was on earth: healings, raising dead people back to life and returning to life Himself.

God's power is available to us, too, if we have even a tiny bit of faith.

Living It

How cool would it be to be able to move a mountain from one spot to another? OK, that might not be something you actually need to do. But how about having enough faith to do miracles that really help people, like Jesus did?

There is an abundance of power available to Jesus' followers – power to do His work in the world and to help people in wonderful ways. A mustard seed is a teeny-tiny seed and just that amount of faith can make a difference. Awesome!

Childlike Humility

The opposite of pride is humility. Pride is all about self. It's a "me, me!" kind of attitude. Humility is about others.

A humble person thinks about others first and cares about what happens to them. Jesus says that kind of attitude is the winner in His kingdom. Children are so good at caring about others. They haven't learned the drive to be number one so they still care about others.

Jesus says to strive for that childlike kind of attitude that trusts Him, wants to please Him and wants to help others.

> "Whoever takes the lowly position of this child is the greatest in the kingdom of heaven."
> Matthew 18:4

Living It

Nina's neighbor, Mrs. Olson, has a dog. Duke isn't a huge dog but he's not a small dog either. Every day Nina sees Mrs. Olson walking Duke and since she is older and a little weak, Duke kind of drags her around.

Now, Nina is afraid of Duke and even a little afraid of Mrs. Olson. One day Nina saw Duke jerk his leash so hard that Mrs. Olson nearly fell. Nina decided right then to get over her fears and offer to walk Duke for her neighbor. Nina put Mrs. Olson and Duke ahead of her fears, and that humility pleases Jesus.

Sharing the Wealth

> "How hard it is for the rich to enter the kingdom of God!"
>
> Mark 10:23

People with a lot of money can buy whatever they need so they need not be dependent on anyone – even God. A healthy relationship with God is one that is submissive to Him and recognizes God as the authority over all things ... even money.

Jesus taught that money and material possessions should be generously shared with others. The rich man Jesus was speaking to here could not do that. Holding too tightly to material possessions makes it hard to serve God.

Living It

Ariana is basically homeless. She and her mom stay at a shelter to have a place to sleep. Ariana wants to go to school more than just about any girl ever has but she doesn't have decent clothes, or money for supplies or to pay the school fees.

Well, she wouldn't have the money except someone from the city has "adopted" her and pays for all she needs for school. In Ariana's mind, that person is a true Christian because they share instead of keeping the money for themselves.

Give Up Worry

Think about this – Jesus says that anything is possible with God.

When Jesus said this He was responding to a statement from His disciples as to who could possibly be saved if rich people couldn't.

But the point is not whether rich or poor is better, the point is that God can do anything – save anyone, help anyone, change anything.

God is God and nothing is impossible for Him!

"All things are possible with God."
Mark 10:27

Living It

Is there some problem occupying your mind and heart right now? Does it seem impossible to solve? Do you think it's highly unlikely that the situation will be settled in a way that makes you happy? In other words, are you giving up on it?

Don't give up. Give it to God. His power, strength and love for you are beyond measure and all things are possible for Him. If He doesn't change the situation, He will change your desires. He will handle it in the way that is best for all concerned! Trust Him.

A Great Servant

"Whoever wants to become great among you must be your servant, and whoever wants to be first must be slave of all."

Mark 10:43-44

To the world this is upside-down thinking. Who would want to be a servant or a slave? Most people dream of being their own boss or being in control of others. So why would Jesus say this?

Well, remember that Jesus is all about relationships and loving others. He encourages His followers to put others' needs before their own – to be a servant to others instead of thinking only of their own desires.

Living It

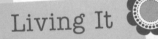

Camryn wants to be popular and to have other girls follow her. She wants others to think she is special. As Camryn works toward this goal, she pushes other girls out of the way and doesn't bother to even talk to anyone who can't help her reach her goal. She will never really have anyone's respect.

Mallory doesn't really care about being popular or having others follow her. But she does care about other girls and looks for ways to help others in any way she can. Mallory will end up with lots of friends who think she is very special.

God's Salt

Once you get used to the taste of salt on your food, anything that isn't salty tastes a little boring. Salt adds flavor and makes food taste good.

Jesus said that His followers are like salt in the world by adding flavor to it.

The flavor that Christians add is the taste of God's love and mercy. His love is deeper and stronger than anything and it is the believer's job to share it with the world.

> "Salt is good, but if it loses its saltiness, how can you make it salty again? Have salt among yourselves, and be at peace with each other."
>
> Mark 9:50

Living It

Celia notices how other girls treat her. Sometimes when a group of girls are talking and laughing and Celia walks up, they suddenly stop. It's not that they aren't friendly, but it seems like their conversation changes when she is around.

Actually, it does because Celia makes them uncomfortable. She is a Christian so her friends feel weird about some of the jokes they tell and the things they say when she is around. Celia is God's salt to the world around her.

Serving Others

"For even the Son of Man did not come to be served, but to serve, and to give His life as a ransom for many."

Mark 10:45

Jesus called for His followers to serve people by putting others' needs and desires ahead of their own. That's not always an easy thing to do. But Jesus doesn't ask His followers to do anything that He doesn't do Himself.

Jesus served others by giving His time and energy to teach and heal the sick. He even raised the dead. Jesus didn't just do what He wanted to do with His time. He gave His time, energy and even His life for others.

Living It

How can you serve others as completely as Jesus did? It could get tiring to spend your time always looking for things to do for others, couldn't it? Start by asking God to open your eyes to ways to serve others. Then be willing to act on what He shows you.

God may show you simple, small ways to help others. As you obey those things, He might show you bigger ways you can serve. Just do what He asks you to do.

True Faith

It sounds so simple, doesn't it. Just have faith in God.

What does it mean to have faith in God? Faith means believing in God's power, strength and love. It means trusting Him to take care of you and to always do what is best for you. It means completely giving yourself over to Him because you know He is in control of absolutely everything and that He loves you more than you can possibly imagine.

Have faith in God and His power is available to you to do incredible things for Him.

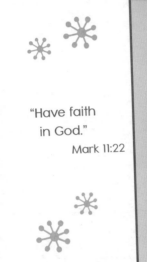

"Have faith in God."
Mark 11:22

Living It

Lucy is quite willing to say, "I believe in God. He's awesome!" But, unfortunately, there isn't much evidence of that in Lucy's life. What's the evidence of lack of faith? She worries about everything and not just a little bit of worry, but worry that sucks the life right out of her.

When Lucy prays it feels as though her prayers bounce off the ceiling right back at her. Why? Because she doesn't really, truly, honestly believe. She doesn't have faith in God. She doesn't really believe in His love, strength, power and love.

Power of Prayer

> "Whatever you ask for in prayer, believe that you have received it, and it will be yours."
>
> Mark 11:24

Do you really believe that God hears your prayers and that He will answer? Prayer is your opportunity to tell Him what's on your heart.

Of course it is important to pray in God's will. What does that mean? Just that it is important to read His Word and make every effort to obey and serve Him. Then, the things you pray for will more likely be things that are good for you.

Just know that, as Jesus says, He will hear your prayers, and yes, He will answer them.

Living It

Trisha read this verse and thought, "Cool. I can get an "A" on my math test and an iPad and ... " Yeah, she didn't quite get it. God is not a big Santa Claus in the sky to give you things or so that you don't have to do your work.

Yes, He wants you to tell Him things you are concerned about. Sometimes His answer may be comfort, and not changing the situation. He wants to hear what you think you need, but most importantly, He wants to give you what is best for you.

Be Honest

Does this seem like a strange warning from Jesus? After all, the teachers of the law were the religious experts of their time so it might seem like they would be the ones who people should respect and obey.

Not really – because Jesus questioned their motives. They liked to be noticed and felt that they were more important than other people. Remember, Jesus sees the heart so He knows why people do what they do.

People like these teachers might fool other people, but Jesus sees that their hearts are full of pride, not love for others.

> "Watch out for the teachers of the law. They like to walk around in flowing robes and be greeted with respect in the marketplaces, and have the most important seats in the synagogues and the places of honor at banquets."
>
> Mark 12:38-39

Living It

Jessica often quotes Bible verses and is the first to offer to pray in Sunday school class. It looks like Jessica is a devoted Christian girl. But what no one knows is that when Jessica is alone she doesn't pray or read her Bible.

Her heart is not devoted to God. She just wants everyone to think that she is. She wants the praise of people without being close to God. She may fool the people around her, but she doesn't fool God because He can see her heart.

Be Careful!

> "Be on your guard;
> I have told you
> everything
> ahead of time."
>
> Mark 13:23

Everything you need to know about living for God is in the Bible.

Jesus has given instructions and challenges to keep you on track. He has also given warnings that there are people who will try to pull you away from serving God. They make up their own rules and try to get others to live by them. They follow their own version of what the Bible teaches. Jesus said to be on the lookout for people who try to pull you away from the truth.

Know what He teaches – know the Bible and you will be just fine.

Living It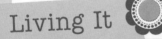

Some kids think the Bible is hard to understand, and some of it is. So, how do you know it well enough to protect yourself and to "be on your guard?" If you read something you don't understand, ask someone you trust what it means.

There are also some versions of the Bible that are easier to understand. Ask God to help you understand His Word. Keep reading and you will keep learning. Be careful about listening to someone who teaches something you know goes against the Bible.

Future Hope

This is so awesome! Jesus is coming back someday! He promises to come back to earth in great power and glory and get His children and take them to heaven with Him!

Whatever problems you face in life will one day be history as you join Jesus in the glory of heaven forever!

Jesus promises to come from heaven and take you there with Him!

> "At that time people will see the Son of Man coming in clouds with great power and glory. And He will send His angels and gather His elect from the four winds, from the ends of the earth to the ends of the heavens."
>
> Mark 13:26-27

Living It

Sometimes Renee gets bogged down with the problems her family has. Renee has some learning disabilities that make school hard. She gets tired of struggling with schoolwork.

Money is always tight so her mom and dad are often stressed and work long hours. Renee wonders if life will ever be easier. This promise from Jesus makes Renee feel better, because she knows that one day everything will be alright because she will be with Jesus and all things in heaven will be good!

Don't Put It Off!

> "Therefore keep watch because you do not know when the owner of the house will come back – whether in the evening, or at midnight, or when the rooster crows, or at dawn. If he comes suddenly, do not let him find you sleeping."
>
> Mark 13:35-36

Pay attention! Jesus warns His followers to pay constant attention to how they are living. No one knows exactly when Jesus will return to earth to get His followers and take them to heaven.

Sometimes people claim to know when Jesus is returning, but they don't really know. The Bible says no one knows.

So, be careful to constantly live for Him and be obedient to Him. Then you will be ready whenever He comes!

Living It

Bekah wants to accept Jesus as her Savior ... someday. Right now she wants to do what she wants and just have fun. She figures she has time to accept Jesus when she is older, but Jesus warns against that attitude.

Bekah must realize that no one knows when Jesus is coming back, so she shouldn't put off accepting Him as Savior. Besides, Bekah can enjoy life now even more with Jesus as her Savior!

Worship First

A woman poured some very expensive perfume on Jesus' feet as she worshiped Him. Some people complained that she was wasting the perfume.

They thought it could be sold and the money given to the poor. At least that's what they said. Jesus stopped their complaints, though, by pointing out that the woman was worshiping Him, which was more than they were doing.

There will always be poor people to help. The woman worshiped Jesus while He was right there with her.

> "The poor you will always have with you, and you can help them any time you want. But you will not always have Me."
>
> Mark 14:7

Living It

It's good to help the poor. In fact, Jesus often said that His followers should share what they have with others. But the act of helping others should never be more important than worshiping Him.

Take time to spend time alone with Jesus and worship Him with no distractions from other things – even good things.

Believing What Jesus Says

"Put out into deep water, and let down the nets for a catch."

Luke 5:4

Jesus said this to some fishermen who had already been out fishing all night, but had caught nothing.

Peter (who became one of Jesus' followers) wanted to argue with Jesus, but he didn't. Peter did what Jesus asked and the result was a catch of fish so big that they could barely pull in the nets.

Jesus blessed Peter beyond his wildest dreams, because Peter believed Him and did what He asked.

Living It

Are you willing to take a chance? If Jesus asked you to do something that seemed like a bit of a stretch for you, would you give it a try?

Sometimes the things Jesus asks seem a bit scary or even strange because you can't see the big picture like He can. Just like Peter, you may be blessed beyond your wildest dreams when you choose to do what He asks!

Making a Way

Jesus came to earth to help people who need Him. God's plan from the minute Adam and Eve sinned was for Jesus to make a way for people to have a personal relationship with Him and to be forgiven of their sins.

God wanted people to come face to face with their sin, then turn away from sin and be able to come to heaven some day. That's why Jesus came to call sinners.

> "I have not come to call the righteous, but sinners to repentance."
> Luke 5:32

Living It

Who are the sinners Jesus came for? You. Actually, everyone. The Bible says that every person is a sinner. Jesus came to call everyone to repentance. That means you need to recognize that you are a sinner (disobey God's laws; are selfish and hurtful toward others).

Confess your sin to God, ask His forgiveness, and invite Him into your heart to be your Savior. There, now Jesus has called you to repentance. Cool, eh?

Prayer

"Everyone who asks receives; the one who seeks finds; and to the one who knocks, the door will be opened."

Luke 11:10

The most amazing gift from God is the Holy Spirit who lives in your heart – guiding your thoughts, actions and prayers.

So, as Jesus taught, when you want to know God and ask for His help in your life, the Holy Spirit guides your prayers.

This means that your prayers will be answered and your understanding of God's work in your life will be deeper.

The more you ask, the more you learn. The more you learn, the more you know.

Living It

"Please God, please, oh please," Maria prayed. She just kept praying the same sentence over and over. Does God know what she is asking Him to do? Yep. Maria has asked Jesus to be her Savior.

Maria has God's Holy Spirit living in her heart. She tries to be obedient to His teachings and is sensitive to the Holy Spirit's guidance in her prayers. Maria loves God. She knows that He loves her.

Being a Witness

It must have made Jesus sad. The people who knew Him best – the ones who watched Him grow from childhood to manhood were the least likely to believe that He was God's true Son.

It is most difficult to convince those closest to you because they know you the best. In Jesus' case, of course, there was nothing bad they could say about Him. Perhaps He was just too familiar.

This is a good reminder for you that the people you care about the most may be the most doubtful about the realness of your relationship with Christ.

> "Truly I tell you," He continued "no prophet is accepted in his hometown."
> Luke 4:24

Living It

Tonya is a new Christian. She is excited about her faith and wants to tell everyone about Jesus. But no one else in her family is, and they don't seem to want to hear anything about her faith. They say stuff like, "You're just showing off. We know the real you who pouts and throws fits and is selfish."

Tonya knows it's going to take a while for them to see that her heart has changed. She will just keep showing them the new Tonya!

Submitting to God

> "Father, everything is possible for You. Take this cup from Me. Yet not what I will, but what You will."
>
> Mark 14:36

Jesus prayed this prayer in the Garden of Gethsemane. He knew what was coming and it wasn't going to be pleasant. He would be tortured and eventually killed.

It was an important part of God's plan that would make salvation possible for people.

Jesus was willing to do what God wanted. He submitted to God and trusted Him and loved you enough to do what God asked Him to.

Living It

Doing hard things is ... hard. Kirsten knows that better than anyone because she isn't especially brave. She isn't courageous at all and will often try to find the easy way out – from school projects to chores to obeying God.

But when Kirsten reads these words of Jesus it makes her feel strong enough to do the right thing, even when it's hard. "Not My will but Yours," she reads. If that's good enough for Jesus, then it's good enough for her! She will try harder, with Jesus helping her!

Watch and Pray!

Jesus was in the Garden of Gethsemane and about to be arrested.

Some of His friends were with Him and He had asked them to watch and pray with Him. They must have seen how stressed He was, but they kept falling asleep instead of praying. They weren't focused on Him so they couldn't stay awake to help Him. That's why Jesus gave this warning: stay focused.

Watch and pray because if you aren't focused, then no matter how hard you try, you will fall into temptation. Satan takes big advantage of that.

> "Watch and pray so that you will not fall into temptation. The spirit is willing, but the flesh is weak."
>
> Mark 14:38

Living It

Betsy wants to be dedicated to spending time with God every day. She promises herself that she will spend a half an hour every day reading the Bible and praying.

For about 2 days Betsy does really well. Then on the third day a friend calls during her quiet time and Betsy talks to her. On the fourth day she falls asleep and on the fifth day something else happens. Eventually Betsy forgets about her promise, and time with God is a forgotten thing. Her spirit was willing, but her body was weak.

Safe and Secure

> "My Father, who has given them to Me, is greater than all; no one can snatch them out of My Father's hand."
>
> John 10:29

What comfort there is in this statement! Jesus is letting everyone know that once you accept Him as Savior, you belong to Him and no one can ever change that.

God is greater and stronger than anyone or anything and that power protects you. Yes, there will be temptations. Yes, there will be problems.

But hold firm to Jesus during all of them because He is holding firm to you!

Living It

Lisa feels safe when she thinks that she belongs to God and that He is the most powerful being in the universe. When life gets tough and it feels like her world is crashing down around her, she doesn't have to worry that God has turned away from her or that Satan is pulling her away from God. It can't happen.

Even with life's problems, Lisa knows that God is taking care of her, strengthening her and guiding her. She is His.

September

Stay Connected

> "Remain in Me, as I also remain in you. No branch can bear fruit by itself; it must remain in the vine. Neither can you bear fruit unless you remain in Me."
>
> John 15:4

Stick close to Jesus. That's where your strength comes from. Jesus points that out by using the example of a vine.

The branches of the vine get their food and water by staying connected to the vine. It's impossible for a branch to grow on its own and be able to produce fruit. That only happens by staying connected to the vine.

The same is true for Christians. You must stay connected to Jesus, who gives you spiritual food and strength. He helps you grow fruit for Him!

Living It

How do you "remain" in Jesus? What does that mean? It means staying connected to Him.

You do that by reading His Word, which teaches you how to obey Him and live for Him. You also stay connected by praying and talking with Him, and then just by being quiet sometimes so that He can speak with you. Only by staying connected to Jesus can you effectively live for Him and do the things He wants you to.

Useful Lives

Following Jesus is serious business. He warns against taking it lightly.

Jesus encourages you to stay close to Him and get your strength from Him. If you don't, you are pretty much useless – like a dead branch that is cut off and thrown away because it has no use.

To be an instrument in God's hand, stay close to Jesus.

> "If you do not remain in Me, you are like a branch that is thrown away and withers; such branches are picked up, thrown into the fire and burned."
>
> John 15:6

Living It

Jesus doesn't walk away from those who don't stay close to Him. He always waits for them to come back.

But a lot of time is wasted when you don't stay close to Him. Time that could be spent learning more about Him, serving Him and encouraging others to get to know Him, too!

Jesus Loves You!

> "As the Father has loved Me, so have I loved you. Now remain in My love."
>
> John 15:9

God loves His only Son very much. His love is complete, sacrificial, and never stops giving.

You know what's amazing? Jesus loves you in the very same way! Isn't that amazing?

He loves you completely, and, of course, sacrificially. His love asks for nothing in return except that you love Him back and stick close to Him.

What an amazing gift – to be loved by Jesus.

Living It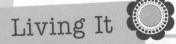

Lainie loves this verse – **Jesus loves her!** What a great thing to know. When she is feeling lonely or sad, she remembers **Jesus loves me!** When she feels happy and wants to celebrate, she remembers **Jesus loves me!**

Lainie is so happy knowing that Jesus loves her. She loves reading the Bible, thinking about Him and even singing about Him. Lainie remains in Jesus' love because she knows He loves her!

True Joy

Jesus wants you to know that the things He teaches in the Bible are not meant to make your life unhappy. They are not a bunch of rules that you have to keep.

Jesus taught the things in the Bible knowing that if you live the way He teaches, you will be filled with joy! Your relationship with God and with others will be good because you will treat others with respect.

Follow Jesus and be filled with complete joy!

"I have told you this so that My joy may be in you and that your joy may be complete."

John 15:11

Living It

Margie has noticed that the more she lives following the way Jesus teaches, the more joy she has. Joy is not the same as happiness. There are times when Margie is not happy because of problems or just feeling down.

But even when she isn't happy, she has an underlying joy because she knows that Jesus loves her and that He is guiding and protecting her.

Love One Another

"My command is this: Love each other as I have loved you."

John 15:12

Jesus is all about love. He encourages His followers to love others unconditionally. Just love.

The love that Jesus shows by His example is unselfish and sacrificial. He holds nothing back from those He loves. Now Jesus commands you to love in the same way He loves.

It isn't always easy to love this way, but you don't have to do it on your own. Jesus helps you love others in ways you never knew you could.

Living It

Love comes pretty easy for Jeanie. She loves most people, but there is one person she has a little trouble with ... Sadie. Jeanie tried to love Sadie, but Sadie is so mean to her.

It's hard for Jeanie to even want nice things to happen for Sadie. So, Jeanie asks God to help her love this difficult friend. Guess what? He does help her! He helps her love Sadie in the same way He loves her!

Proof for Doubters

Jesus knew that the hardest people to convince that He was truly the Messiah, the Son of God, were the religious people.

So, when He healed a man who had leprosy – a terrible skin disease, He told the man to keep quiet about it until he had told the priest and offered the sacrifices that were required.

He wanted the man to do everything by the book so that the priest would have to admit that a miracle had taken place and that Jesus was the reason.

> "Don't tell anyone, but go, show yourself to the priest and offer the sacrifices that Moses commanded for your cleansing, as a testimony to them."
>
> Luke 5:14

Living It

People who think they know everything are the hardest to convince that they may not have all the answers. Linnie has seen this firsthand. Her older brother thinks he knows pretty much everything and that there is no place in His life for God.

In fact, he's bitter toward God, though no one knows why. So, Linnie takes every opportunity to give credit to God when she can and just prays that her faithfulness to Him will be noticed by her brother. She is a testimony to her brother of God's work in her life.

You Get What You Give

> "Do not judge, and you will not be judged. Do not condemn, and you will not be condemned. Forgive, and you will be forgiven."
>
> Luke 6:37

Treat other people the way you want to be treated. That's not so hard, is it? Well, it shouldn't be, but unfortunately it sometimes is.

Jesus made a point (a couple of times) that it's important to treat others the way you want to be treated ... even by God.

Why should you expect Him to forgive you, not condemn you or judge you if you can't treat other people in that same manner?

Think about how you treat others because it matters.

Living It

This Scripture verse makes so much sense to Lydia because when she asks God to forgive her for something, the first thing that comes to mind is a friend she's been holding a grudge against.

Yeah, that's God reminding her to forgive others before she asks Him to forgive her. That's how it works.

Follow the Leader

Jesus often warned people to be careful of those they were listening to and who they were following.

Why? Because if you listen to someone who doesn't really know any more than you (even if she acts like she does), then you aren't going to get good guidance and help. Yep, it would be like a blind man leading another across a busy eight-lane highway ... gulp.

Choose the wisest, most loving person to follow ... Jesus.

> "Can the blind lead the blind? Will they not both fall into a pit?"
> Luke 6:39

Living It

For some reason most of the girls in Sandy's class think Ariana is super cool. They do what she says and think what she thinks. They try to be like her in every way. Sandy doesn't get it. Ariana doesn't always make good choices and sometimes she is just downright mean, which means the other girls are also mean.

Ariana doesn't have life completely figured out. After all, she is just a kid, too. Sandy chooses to follow Jesus by learning His teaching and seeking His guidance in her life.

Eye Trouble

"Why do you look at the speck of sawdust in your brother's eye and pay no attention to the plank in your own eye?"

Luke 6:41

It is so easy to criticize others – especially when a group of girls get together and start picking on one person.

Jesus raises the question of why this happens. After all, no one is perfect.

Every single person is a sinner. Why judge someone for some small fault you see when you have huge problems with your own behavior?

Seriously, it's probably true that whatever bugs you in another girl's behavior is a problem because it's something you struggle with, too.

Living It

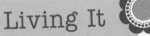

"You complain about **everything**," Annie complained. Chrissie just shook her head and walked away. Yeah, she had been complaining again. And she was complaining about the same old thing. But, truth be told, she did not complain nearly as much as Annie. If you spent time with her, you would think Annie didn't like anything or anyone! So, just as Jesus said, Annie complained about the speck of dust in Chrissie's eye when she had a whole log in her own! Take care of your own problems before you complain about someone else's.

Total Sharing

Complete unselfishness is what Jesus requests of His followers. He encourages you to be so focused on helping others that you do not hold anything back from sharing with them.

Jesus wants His followers to be so aware of people's needs, that, should someone take something that belongs to you because they really need it, you do not ask for it back.

If Jesus had His way, no one would go hungry and no one would be homeless because those who had food and money would share with the poor.

"Give to everyone who asks you, and if anyone takes what belongs to you, do not demand it back."
Luke 6:30

Living It

Lucy tries hard to understand Jesus' call to be totally unselfish. It isn't always easy, but she prays for His help to have an open mind. Lucy really cares about others. When Lucy hears of people who don't have enough food or water or children who don't have any toys or books, she wants to help.

She is even willing to give her own stuff away, even new stuff. She always has more than she needs, so why not share with others? It's the Jesus thing to do!

What's Inside Counts

> "No good tree bears bad fruit, nor does a bad tree bear good fruit."
>
> Luke 6:43

Everyone makes bad choices sometimes. Everyone makes mistakes. A girl who has asked Jesus to be her Savior has the love of Jesus in her heart.

In this example that Jesus gives, that girl would be a good tree and she would bear beautiful fruit. That means she loves God and others.

People are able to see that Jesus is in her heart by the way she lives.

Living It

Kerry knows good fruit comes from a healthy tree. Her grandmother is the kindest, most loving person Kerry has ever met.

Her grandmother always says that God has done so much for her that His love just overflows her heart and spills out to others. She is an amazing example to Kerry of sharing God's love with others.

Getting Rid of the Junk

Life will not be problem-free just because you ask Jesus to be your Savior. In fact, sometimes you may feel like you have more than your share of problems.

Jesus actually promises that some of the difficult times will be to help you grow in your relationship with Him.

Does that sound harsh? It may be difficult, but stay focused on what you can learn from the difficulties.

> "He cuts off every branch in Me that bears no fruit, while every branch that does bear fruit He prunes so that it will be even more fruitful."
>
> John 15:2

Living It

Bonnie didn't understand it. Was God going to send bad things into her life? Well, He allows things to happen sometimes that will make you choose to follow Him or not. Those choices help you realize whether or not you are focused on Him. That helps you grow, because you get practice in choosing the Jesus way.

Just as a gardener cuts off dead branches from a tree, the choices you make cut dead areas out of your life. You come out stronger after the problems are settled.

Obey and Love

God's love for you is free, but it comes with an insistence that you return His love and make every effort to obey Him.

Deliberately disobeying God makes a break in your relationship with Him. Jesus is your example. He obeyed God, even when it was difficult.

But, because He obeyed He knew that He and God were close and that He could rest in God's love.

Living It

Obeying is not always easy. A lot of things and people around you tell you not to obey God. They tell you that obeying is just a bunch of rules. What they don't know is that obeying God is proof that you love Him and are working on learning to love Him even more.

The more you love God, the more you know you can depend on Him. He loves you even more than you love Him and He will take care of you ... always.

No Greater Love

Jesus showed His love for you in a way that is unlike anything else! He said that the greatest evidence of someone's love for you would be if he is willing to give his own life for yours.

Jesus did. Yes, He died for you so you can be free of your sins.

He also dedicated His life on this earth to teaching and loving you!

> "Greater love has no one than this: to lay down one's life for one's friends."
>
> John 15:13

Living It

OK, does this mean that you need to die to show that you love your friends? No, of course not. So how do you "lay down your life for a friend?"

Take all selfishness and self-centeredness out of your life and dedicate yourself to serving and helping others. Make others your focus instead of yourself. You have a great example to follow – Jesus focused His daily life on teaching, loving and helping others. Follow His example!

Friendship

> "I no longer call you servants, because a servant does not know his master's business. Instead, I have called you friends, for everything that I learned from My Father I have made known to you."
>
> John 15:15

Look at the relationship described in this statement. Jesus takes your relationship with Him from the master-servant level to a friendship.

What does that mean? A servant only knows information that her master chooses to share. A servant does what she is told to do. A friend knows personal information. A friend is more of an equal.

Jesus wants a close relationship with you – a friendship.

Living It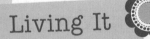

Kristin has really good friends. She knows what a healthy friendship is like. When she reads that Jesus considers her a friend, Kristin gets really excited.

It's much easier to love a friend than it is to love a master. Kristin is very thankful that Jesus is her friend and that He shares everything God taught Him with her. This is real friendship!

Simplicity

Does this mean that Jesus is going to magically fill your closet with cool clothes that all the other girls will be jealous of? Of course not. It means that He will take care of you. He will make sure you have what you need.

That isn't the same as having what you want. These words are a reminder that you can trust Jesus to provide for you.

"Why do you worry about clothes? See how the flowers of the field grow. They do not labor or spin. Yet I tell you that not even Solomon in all his splendor was dressed like one of these."

Matthew 6:28-29

Living It

Girls can be cruel. Cassie has been the victim of some of that cruelty because of the way she dresses. She doesn't have the "right" brand of jeans or sweaters. Her shoes are sneakers from a discount store. Some of the girls in her class make fun of her because of this. At first Cassie was really hurt by their words, but now she doesn't really care. She focuses on what's really important – that she has what she really needs. Her family doesn't have a lot of money, but somehow God always provides for them. Praise the Lord!

God's Word Is Truth

> "Watch out for false prophets. They come to you in sheep's clothing, but inwardly they are ferocious wolves."
>
> Matthew 7:15

Jesus warns against listening to people who teach things that don't agree with what He teaches.

Some people think they know the right way, but if you look at how they live their lives and how they treat other people, you will see that their lives do not reflect Jesus or His love. Often they have taken only parts of Jesus' teaching to obey, instead of the whole Bible.

Living It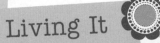

Josie's parents have always encouraged her to read her Bible daily. They have a family Bible study time, too. They know it is important to know God's Word because that is total truth.

The Word of God guards their hearts against false teachers – even those who make their way sound wonderfully appealing. Truth is the best way!

Good Thoughts

Jesus was speaking to some religious teachers who were criticizing His work. It's pretty sad because they were focused on rules instead of people.

Since their hearts were not filled with love, they were consumed with wanting Jesus and others to obey their rules.

Since they didn't, the teachers' hearts were judgmental and critical.

> "Why do you entertain evil thoughts in your hearts?"
> Matthew 9:4

Living It

Anne's heart is filled with evil thoughts. She gets so angry and frustrated and sometimes she doesn't even know why. But a big part of her problem is that she focuses on herself and how everything affects her.

When others don't seem to be thinking about her, Anne has bad thoughts about them. Anne knows she should let Jesus fill her heart with love for others, and stop thinking about herself so much. Good thoughts of love are much better.

No Secret Christians

"Whoever acknowledges Me before others, I will also acknowledge before My Father in heaven."

Matthew 10:32

There is no such thing as a secret Christian.

It is a part of a Christian's honor to be able to share the love of God with other people – so that people everywhere can hear of God's love. The openness of your faith, which spills out of a heart devoted to God, shows God's love to others.

Jesus honors this faith by acknowledging you to God as one of His own.

Living It

Maddie is shy, super shy. She is often worried about what others think about her. So the idea of telling someone about her faith in Jesus makes her knees shake. She doesn't know what to say. But she discovers that it really isn't so hard.

Maddie takes a minute, say a silent thank You prayer at lunch. She simply tells a friend that she goes to church. It's a step-by-step acknowledgement of her faith. One day a friend may ask her more about it and she will be able to see how much Jesus means to Maddie!

The Spirit Leads

When Jesus was ready to go back to heaven He promised that God would send the Holy Spirit to live in believers' hearts and to be with them always and always.

Anytime you don't quite know what is right or wrong, the Spirit will lead you. Jesus promised that the Holy Spirit would help you remember all that Jesus taught.

> "The Advocate, the Holy Spirit, whom the Father will send in My name, will teach you all things and will remind you of everything I have said to you."
>
> John 14:26

Living It

Audrey wonders how the Spirit is going to lead. She says, "I know He doesn't email or text. He doesn't write messages on the wall. How do I know when the Spirit is leading me?"

Well, Audrey, you know that feeling you get inside sometimes when you wonder what to do? There's a little voice in your mind or a feeling inside that says, "Do this" or "Don't do that." That's the Spirit and sometimes He even reminds you of a Bible verse you have read that will help you know right from wrong!

Life Purpose

> "Come, follow Me," Jesus said, "and I will send you out to fish for people."
>
> Matthew 4:19

Jesus called His disciples to follow Him and have a new purpose in their lives. They would have the same purpose He had – to bring people to faith in Jesus. He would show them how.

Jesus-followers today still have that same purpose. As you follow Jesus, He will show you how to lead others to faith in Him.

Jesus used the fishing example in talking with His disciples because they were fishermen. Look for Him to use ways you are familiar with, also.

Living It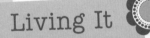

Jenny plays soccer. She is on two different teams so she spends a lot of time at practices and games and she has made some good friends between her two teams.

Jenny follows Jesus' instructions and looks for ways to gently share her faith, even just by the way she lives and behaves, with her soccer friends. They notice.

Thinking of Others

Jesus knew that the world gives a lot of power and authority to powerful, strong and wealthy people. He made it plain that none of those things are especially important to God.

Jesus wasn't giving honor to poor people – but to the poor in spirit. That means humble people who show kindness, respect and honor to others. That is a spirit that reflects Jesus.

> "Blessed are the poor in spirit, for theirs is the kingdom of heaven."
> Matthew 5:3

Living It

Sara has a kind and gentle spirit. She started a program among her friends and classmates to do nice things for the children of prison inmates. She collects winter hats, mittens and warm socks for them ... with an occasional toy thrown in for fun.

Sara notices people who are lonely or left out. She doesn't just notice, she does something about it. Sara thinks of others before herself and that makes God happy.

Better Than Everyone Else?

"Rejoice and be glad, because great is your reward in heaven, for in the same way they persecuted the prophets who were before you."

Matthew 5:12

Jesus knew that some people would not take kindly to the truth that they are sinners. They would get angry when this fact pointed that out and would be mean to the one who delivered that message. Jesus knew this, because it happened to Him.

The good news is right at the beginning of this statement – your reward is in heaven. Jesus is paying attention. He knows what's happening and He will reward His faithful followers.

Living It

"There's old 'Betty-than-everyone-else,'" someone whispered as Betty walked down the hallway. Just because Betty took her faith in Jesus seriously and sometimes refused to join in certain activities or conversations, some of the kids had given her that nickname. It hurt. She would admit that.

Betty didn't think she was better than anyone else. She was just trying to be the best Betty she could be. So, she kept right on living as she always had because she knew it was right and she knew that Jesus knew. That was good enough for her.

Going the Extra Mile

There should be a marked difference between how a Christian treats others and how someone who doesn't know Christ treats others. Jesus says to go the extra mile. That means whatever a person asks of you, do that and even more.

Surprise people with your generosity, helpfulness and kindness. And make sure they know that it comes from a heart focused on loving and obeying Jesus.

"If anyone forces you to go one mile, go with them two miles."
Matthew 5:41

Living It

"I will really appreciate it if any of you can stay after class and help stack up the chairs," Krissy's teacher said. An after-school activity needed the whole floor open in their classroom. When the bell rang, all the kids dashed out the door, eager to get home. Krissy stayed behind and began stacking chairs with the teacher. After a while the teacher said, "Thanks for your help, Krissy, but you can go now." But Krissy didn't leave, she stayed until every chair was stacked. The teacher knows Krissy is a Christian and now she has seen more evidence of that in Krissy's life.

No Strings Attached

> "Give to the one who asks you, and do not turn away from the one who wants to borrow from you."
>
> Matthew 5:42

A generous heart is an unselfish heart. Jesus encourages you to be generous to all people.

Don't hold on to your possessions as though they are more important than people.

Nothing is more important than people. So be generous to all, and do not worry about being repaid.

Living It

Lizzie considers herself a generous person and she really is ... with her friends. But when her brother wants to borrow something, especially one of her favorite books, Lizzie has an issue. "Come on, you loan them to your friends all the time," he whines. It isn't that Lizzie thinks he won't take care of it or return it. It's just that he is such a pain sometimes. She could loan him the book and ask for something in return. But the right thing to do – the Jesus thing to do – is loan him the book, with no strings attached.

Fear or Trust?

You would think that Jesus' disciples would have really strong faith. After all, they were with Him when He healed people and when He raised the dead back to life. They were there when He fed the 5,000 with five fish and two loaves of bread. They knew He could do pretty much anything!

However, they were people just like you and sometimes they got scared that Jesus wasn't going to take care of them.

It must have made Jesus sad that their faith wasn't stronger since they knew so much about Him.

> "You of little faith, why are you so afraid?"
> Matthew 8:26

Living It

Think about this – the disciples lived with Jesus for three and a half years and saw all that He did. Yet, their faith wasn't able to keep them from being afraid sometimes. You have the entire Bible to read that tells you everything He did in that time. So is your faith stronger than theirs?

You may still get scared sometimes. You may occasionally wonder where He is. That's OK, just go back to the Bible and read about His strength, power and love for you. Then, ask Him to help you trust Him more and more.

Desperation Prayers

"Take heart, daughter," Jesus said, "your faith has healed you."

Matthew 9:22

When problems and crises come, many people start praying. They ask God to solve their problems and fix their situations. They may be surprised when He doesn't answer their prayers.

But here is the key – faith. Spouting a prayer when life gets tough but having no relationship with Jesus before or after that prayer is not faith in action. It is desperation.

Faith is what healed the woman Jesus was speaking to here – not desperation.

Living It

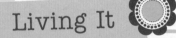

Molly's parents are getting a divorce. They've made the arrangements. It is going to happen. Molly is desperate to stop it. She loves both her parents and doesn't want their family to split up. Molly has never prayed before, but she begins begging God to fix the problem. "Make them love each other again. Stop the divorce!" But it doesn't happen and the divorce goes through. Does this mean God doesn't care? No. He cares a lot. But what He cares about most is having a relationship with Molly, one where she talks with Him often, reads His Word and learns to trust Him.

As You Go ...

Jesus often spoke about the work He has for His followers. That work is to tell others about the love of God and help them find a way to know and follow Him.

The cool thing about this statement is that Jesus trusts His followers will obediently do the work. He says, "As you go ..." so He expects your obedience in telling others.

> "As you go, proclaim this message: 'The kingdom of heaven has come near.'"
>
> Matthew 10:7

Living It

Abby wants to be obedient to Jesus but, she doesn't know how to tell others about Him. She isn't exactly sure what "the kingdom of heaven is near" means. So, she asks her pastor for advice. He said, "Abby, let your friends know that you do love Jesus. Tell them that He is important to you. Live your life so they can see His values. As far as the kingdom of heaven being near ... it is. It's close to you because Jesus lives in your heart and one day soon He will come back to earth to get His family and take us to heaven with Him. Make sure your friends know that, too!"

God-Speak

"It will not be you speaking, but the Spirit of your Father speaking through you."

Matthew 10:20

There will be times when people attack your faith and you simply do not know how to defend yourself or your God.

Jesus said to stay super close to God and to rely on the Holy Spirit in those times. He will give you the right words. He will help you to be courageous but respectful, strong but kind and His words will actually be the words of God, spoken through your lips!

Living It

Maddie's science teacher does not believe in God or the Bible. He is absolutely certain that evolution is true and that God had nothing to do with the creation of anything. He gets really sarcastic with any learner who challenges him or even mentions God. Maddie wants to state her case for faith in God, but she is scared. She doesn't know what to say. So, she follows Jesus' advice and asks God to give her the right words and the right time. Guess what? He does! She respectfully but strongly states her faith in Jesus and the truth of the Bible!

Fence Riders

This is serious business. Jesus warns people not to take their relationship with Him too lightly. If you sit on the fence – not committing but not denying your belief in Jesus, you can be sure the day will come when you will have to take a stand.

> "Whoever disowns Me before others, I will disown before My Father in heaven."
> Matthew 10:33

If you deny Jesus because you're too embarrassed or scared to say you believe, then don't expect Him to stick up for you, either.

Get in or get out – there is no riding the fence here.

Living It

Marsha tries to keep everyone happy. When she is with her Christian friends, she talks about God, prays before her meals, promises to pray for friends' problems. She knows all the lingo and the right actions and she does every one.

But when she is with her non-Christian friends, all that goes out the window. She speaks and behaves just like they do and proclaims that she wants nothing to do with God! She tries to have it both ways. Guess what? That won't work. Take a stand for Jesus, Marsha!

October

Bearing Witness

> "Go back and report to John what you hear and see: The blind receive sight, the lame walk, those who have leprosy are cleansed, the deaf hear, the dead are raised, and the good news is proclaimed to the poor."
>
> Matthew 11:4-5

Jesus instructed people to bear witness to His work. Just as a witness in a court case testifies of what she has seen or heard, a witness of Jesus' work testifies of His work so that others may believe in His strength and power.

Then they will believe that He is God's Son and that He came to earth to show love for mankind and make a way for people to know God.

Living It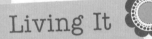

"How do you know Jesus is real?" Cindy asked Debbie. "Seriously, the Bible could just be a bunch of stories. How do you know it's true?"

Debbie had an answer. She could testify of Jesus' work in her life and the wonderful answers to her prayers and how He directed and guided her. Debbie bears witness to Jesus' work so that Cindy will know He is real!

Smooth Talkers

Jesus is speaking to smooth talkers. You know the type – they know exactly the right things to say, but Jesus knows there is no sincerity in their words.

They may say things that make them appear to honor and love God, but their hearts are far away from Him. Eventually the wickedness and evil in their hearts comes out in their lives.

Remember, Jesus sees your heart and while you can fool people, you can never fool God.

"You brood of vipers, how can you who are evil say anything good? For the mouth speaks what the heart is full of."

Matthew 12:34

Living It

Lacey knows a few smooth talkers. One girl in particular acts like she is Lacey's best friend just so she can get information she wants. Then her real personality comes out and she's not very nice.

Lacey is reminded to pay attention to how people live and notice whether their lives match the kind and concerned words they speak. If they don't, then she knows that that person is a smooth talker whose heart does not belong to Jesus.

Baby Steps

"Whoever does the will of My Father in heaven is My brother and sister and mother."

Matthew 12:50

People who obey God and serve Him become His family members. Jesus did not dismiss His earthly family – He asked a friend to take care of His mother before He died.

In this verse, He was emphasizing how close He is to His obedient followers. They become family to Him. How cool is that?

Obeying God makes you a family member, too!

Living It

Lizzie thinks obeying all the things Jesus teaches in the Bible is a really big job. How can one little girl obey all those things? She wants to be obedient to Jesus. She wants to be in His family, but it is overwhelming! How can she do it?

One way for Lizzie to get started is to begin with one thing, like honoring her mom and dad as Jesus teaches her to do. Then work on loving others more than herself. Lizzie understands now that doing God's will begins by learning one thing at a time.

Secrets!

Jesus was speaking to normal, everyday people when He said this. He was not speaking to the arrogant, know-it-all religious leaders who criticized His every move.

Isn't it cool that the secrets of heaven are given to normal people who have humble and seeking hearts – who want to know Him better?

The religious leaders who thought they had all the answers would not understand the messages of Jesus' stories because their hearts didn't want to know God better. They just wanted to be in control, even of Jesus. That didn't happen.

"The knowledge of the secrets of the kingdom of heaven has been given to you, but not to them."
Matthew 13:11

Living It

"I'm just a kid," Haley thought, "so how can I understand the lessons of the Bible? I really love Jesus and I want to be closer and closer to Him, but I'm just a kid." Haley is so much closer than she thinks!

Having a heart that desires to know God puts her miles ahead of someone who thinks she has all the answers. Haley's seeking heart is the heart to which God will reveal the deeper meanings of Scripture.

A Calloused Heart

> "For this people's heart has become calloused; they hardly hear with their ears, and they have closed their eyes. Otherwise they might see with their eyes, hear with their ears, understand with their hearts and turn, and I would heal them."
>
> Matthew 13:15

A calloused heart is one that has grown a thick, hard-to-penetrate shell around it. It cares only for itself and can't be touched with the truth of God's Word or care for other people. It's a sad condition, which will separate the person from God.

It isn't hopeless, though. If this person could open her heart to Jesus, He would heal that calloused heart and she would be able to see and hear the truth of His love.

Living It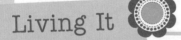

Bailey has been praying for her friend Caylie to come to know Jesus. Caylie has heard the message of Jesus' love. She has talked with Bailey about her faith, but she says it just doesn't make any sense to her.

Bailey thinks Caylie's heart might be calloused, just like this verse says. Now Bailey prays for Jesus' love to break through that thick skin on Caylie's heart so that she can understand how very much Jesus loves her!

Complete Surrender

You can't follow Jesus and hold some part of yourself back from Him. Complete surrender – giving up all your life – means surrendering your wants, hopes, dreams, time, activities and passions to Jesus.

Later He teaches you what He wants you to do, how He wants you to live, how He wants you to treat others, and how to love Him and others.

So, while it may seem as though you are giving up your life, or at least control of your life, you are actually gaining the joy of living for Jesus and the promise of eternal life with Him!

> "Whoever wants to save their life will lose it, but whoever loses their life for Me will find it."
>
> Matthew 16:25

Living It

When Andie asked Jesus to be her Savior, she meant it and she really intended to follow Him. But there was one part of her life that she just couldn't give up control of – her friendships. There were a couple of girls who were important friends to Andie, even though they often dragged her into activities that were disrespectful and not of God.

Until Andie can give God that part of her life, too, she will not be completely surrendered to God and will not find her new life.

Childlike Faith

> "Truly I tell you, unless you change and become like little children, you will never enter the kingdom of heaven."
>
> Matthew 18:3

Powerful, important, strong people do not impress Jesus. People who think they have all the answers are not dependent on Him. They don't think they need Him.

Children who are dependent and trusting and who desire to honor Jesus by obeying Him are the ones who please Him. Jesus points out that these little children have a place in heaven.

Living It

Keshia trusts Jesus. Once she accepted Jesus as Savior, she quickly began to feel like Jesus was her best friend. She wanted to spend time with Him and get to know Him better and better.

Keshia knows she doesn't have all the answers to life. She knows she needs to learn from Jesus and she can't wait to do that!

Role Model Responsibilities

Jesus knew that people have the influence to cause others to sin. That's true even of kids.

You have influence over others, especially someone who is younger and looks up to you.

If you lead another girl to do something wrong; either by encouraging her to do it or by showing her how to do it; you will answer to Jesus for it.

"Woe to the world because of the things that cause people to stumble! Such things must come, but woe to the person through whom they come!"
Matthew 18:7

Living It

Lara is a couple of years younger than Zoe and looks up to her as a role model. Lara does whatever Zoe does, so when she heard Zoe and her friends making fun of a new girl in school, Lara started doing the same thing. She picked on the girl's clothes, hairstyle, intelligence and whatever else she could think of. Lara thought she was being cool like Zoe. She was wrong. She was being mean to someone she didn't even know. Both Zoe and Lara will have to answer to Jesus for their words, but Zoe even more so for leading Lara down that path.

Special Jane!

> "In the same way your Father in heaven is not willing that any of these little ones should not perish."
>
> Matthew 18:14

Jesus was explaining to His disciples how much God loves all people.

He pulled a small child into the room and explained that just as a shepherd would leave 99 sheep on a hillside to go find one sheep that had wandered away, there is a party in heaven each time one person accepts Jesus.

This verse was the closing of that example – God wants every single person, adult and child to know Him.

Living It

Jane never felt special. She was right in the middle of a family of six children so she often got lost in the shuffle. She wasn't especially good at anything. She was an average student, average singer, average athlete, average conversationalist. She was ... average.

But, when her heart began to understand that God wanted her to know Him, she felt anything but average! For the first time in her life, Jane felt special!

Prayer Partners

Is Jesus saying that there is power in numbers? Not necessarily. Is He saying that if you get a friend to join you He will give you **anything** you want? Nope. Well, then, what is He saying?

Jesus is emphasizing how good it is to share your prayer requests with others. There is comfort in knowing that someone else is praying with you about something important – and even praying together.

It is still important for all who pray to be close to God so that He can guide their prayers.

> "I tell you that if two of you on earth agree about anything they ask for, it will be done for them by My Father in heaven."
>
> Matthew 18:19

Living It

Sada is carrying a heavy load all by herself. Her best friend dumped her to be besties with someone else. Sada feels like a loser and is very, very lonely.

Debbie is Sada's Sunday school teacher. She notices how sad Sada is so she asks her what's wrong. Sada tells her how lonely she is and they begin praying together for a new friend for Sada. Just knowing that someone else is praying with her makes Sada feel better and before long, she has lots of friends!

Don't Go it Alone!

> "For where two or three gather in My name, there am I with them."
>
> Matthew 18:20

Jesus is all about relationships. The Christian life is not intended to be lived by yourself, separate from all others.

Jesus encourages people of similar beliefs and passions to join together in prayer, worship and service to Him.

One person can accomplish some things, but a group of people can encourage one another and help one another to accomplish so much more!

Living It

Lisa's heart aches for the children in the homeless shelters. They really touch her heart and she wants to do something for them. But what? There are so many of them and she is just one person. Then, Lisa has an idea. She enlists the help of her friends and their parents. They hold garage sales and hire themselves out to do work for neighbors. All the money they earn is used to buy winter coats, mittens and hats, and one small toy for each child. Lisa is so happy that her friends have helped. She could never have done all this by herself.

Forgiveness

Peter had just asked Jesus how many times he had to forgive someone who had wronged him. Peter thought seven times of forgiveness was good. Jesus disagreed with him.

Seventy-seven times seems like a lot of forgiveness, doesn't it? That's the point. Forgive and forgive and forgive, because that's what Jesus does for you.

Forgive over and over to the point that you lose count, because keeping score is not the point. Forgiveness and restoring the relationship is.

> "I tell you, not seven times, but seventy-seven times."
> Matthew 18:22

Living It

"She thinks she is so funny. Her slams hurt and I'm sick and tired of it!" Ella said to her Mom. "I'll never forgive Kelly. I'm so done with her." Mom listened quietly, then said, "Maybe she doesn't know she is hurting you. Why don't you talk to her. You've been friends a long time" "Yeah," Ella interrupted, "and I've forgiven her like a billion times. No more!"

"Ella, forgiveness doesn't have a limit. Kelly is your friend. Talk with her and give her another chance, just like she does for you; and especially like God does for you," Mom said.

No Memory

> "The servant's master took pity on him, canceled the debt and let him go."
>
> Matthew 18:27

Jesus gave an example of true forgiveness by telling the story of a man who owed money to a king but was unable to pay it back.

The man fell on his knees and begged the king's forgiveness. He asked for the king's patience and promised to pay back every cent. The king had mercy on him and canceled the debt completely and let him go!

True forgiveness forgets as well as forgives. The debt is completely gone.

Living It

"I'm sorry, Lila. I know it was wrong to say what I did and I know it hurt you. Please forgive me," Cindra quietly said. Lila thought about it for a few minutes and finally, grudgingly said, "OK, I forgive you." But you know what? She didn't! She filed away this hurt by Cindra in the back of her mind. Someday, when she needed ammunition, she would pull it out and stick it back in Cindra's face. Guess what? That's not forgiveness. Forgiving and forgetting is the mark of true forgiveness – not forgiving to have ammunition for the future!

Forgive as You Are Forgiven

Jesus told this story of a king who forgave one of his servants who was indebted to him. Then the servant turned around and had another man thrown in jail for a small debt owed to him.

Where is the justice in that? Since the man received grace for a big debt, why didn't he offer the other man grace for a small debt?

The bottom line is to forgive others because you have been forgiven.

"Shouldn't you have had mercy on your fellow servant just as I had on you?"
Matthew 18:33

Living It

Haley broke her mother's beautiful crystal angel. She felt terrible. It had belonged to Grandma and Haley knew it was very special to her mother. Haley apologized and asked her forgiveness. Her mom was very sad to have lost this gift from her mother, but she forgave Haley. Later that night Haley's brother accidentally broke a pencil he had borrowed from her. Haley went crazy, yelling at him and promising to get even. Hayley's mother then reminded her that she had forgiven her for something big, so Haley should consider forgiving her brother. Mom was right. As usual.

Sincere Forgiveness

> "This is how My heavenly Father will treat each of you unless you forgive your brother or sister from your heart."
>
> Matthew 18:35

This is how Jesus ended His story about the man who was forgiven for his large debt and then refused to forgive someone who owed him a little bit of money.

Jesus said that God notices this kind of selfishness. Don't ask God to forgive you if you refuse to truly and honestly forgive others.

In Jesus' story, the unforgiving man is tortured and thrown into jail. Not a pretty picture, is it?

Living It

Alison was very, very angry at Fran. She wanted to hurt her. She wanted to make all their friends mad at Fran, too. Instead, Fran asked Alison to forgive her. She said she was sorry for what she had done. So Alison said she would forgive Fran, but she didn't mean it. Alison still had a lot of anger in her heart and she still tried to get their friends on her side, and against Fran. Alison's friends were frustrated with her for not being honest and they all turned away from her. Forgiveness must be sincere or it isn't forgiveness at all.

Eternal Life

God is in a category all by Himself. What respect, honor and worship He commands!

Jesus made this statement to a rich man who asked Him how to get eternal life. Jesus quickly pointed out the necessity of recognizing God's goodness and giving Him the honor He deserves.

Because of that honor you should obey the commandments God has given and learn that respect, honor and obedience leads to eternal life.

> "Why do you ask Me about what is good?" Jesus replied. "There is only One who is good. If you want to enter life, keep the commandments."
>
> Matthew 19:17

Living It

"Yeah, I want to have eternal life. I'm just a kid now but I'd like to know that someday I'm going to heaven," Ellie says.

But is Ellie willing to commit to recognizing God as the only one who is truly good? The only one who is perfect and sinless and loving and kind and honest and fair? Is Ellie willing to learn His commandments that are given in the Bible and to obey them? Those are necessary things to receiving eternal life and living for Jesus. Ellie needs to make the choice to honor and obey God.

Thinking of Others

> "'You shall not murder, you shall not commit adultery, you shall not steal, you shall not give false testimony, honor your father and mother,' and 'love your neighbor as yourself.'"
>
> Matthew 19:18-19

Jesus reviews six of the Ten Commandments here ... the six that involve how you treat others. He reviews them for a wealthy man who asks what commandments he needs to obey to obtain eternal life.

It's interesting that Jesus mentioned the commandments about relating to other people rather than the ones that focus on how to relate to God.

Jesus knew that face-to-face relationships would be even harder to maintain than a spiritual relationship with Christ. However, it's important to have healthy relationships with others.

Living It

"I'm good," thought Carol. "I haven't murdered anyone or committed adultery or stolen anything." Yep, Carol thought she was doing pretty good. However, she conveniently skipped over the command to honor her father and mother.

Her temper tantrum last night didn't cross her mind. She got angry because her mom made her do chores. And the last command, to love her neighbor as herself, well, that one she wasn't always so good at, either. Carol needs to read the whole list – not just the easy ones.

Selling to Help

This is Jesus' final answer to the rich man who wanted to know how to find eternal life. Jesus focused the man's attention on caring for others.

People can divide their hearts so that with one part they praise God, speak about loving Him, and obey Him. But with the other part they disregard people, holding on to their possessions, and showing that they do not care for others at all.

Caring for people is important to Jesus. He makes that crystal clear.

> "If you want to be perfect, go, sell your possessions and give to the poor, and you will have treasure in heaven. Then come, follow Me."
>
> Matthew 19:21

Living It

Ruthie got it. She understood what Jesus meant by giving to the poor. Ruthie organized a garage sale in her neighborhood with some of her friends. She encouraged them to sell things: nice things, things that they liked.

She said, "We have so much stuff and there are some kids who don't even have warm clothes. Let's sell our stuff to raise money to buy things other kids need." Ruthie's friends joined in and they sold enough to raise $500 to give to a mission that helps kids.

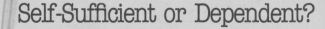

Self-Sufficient or Dependent?

"Truly I tell you, it is hard for someone who is rich to enter the kingdom of heaven."

Matthew 19:23

Why would Jesus say this? Aren't rich people important and powerful? Don't they get whatever they want?

Wealthy people are often important and powerful and sometimes feel that they can get whatever they want.

Rich people may not see the need to depend on God or trust Him for their needs. That's why it is hard for a rich person to enter heaven.

Living It

What's wrong with getting what you want? Nothing really. But Jesus' point is that to be in God's family, you need to trust Him completely.

The reason it's hard for people with a lot of money to do that is that they expect to get what they want because they can buy it. They expect others to listen to them because their money gives them power. But God doesn't do what anyone tells Him to do. Coming to faith in Jesus takes a certain kind of humility and sometimes that is hard for wealthy people.

The First Shall be Last

Powerful, important, decision-makers, famous, influential, wealthy. These are all words that describe people who are used to being first. They are used to being respected, honored and getting their way.

The people who are usually last are poorer, quieter, more humble, sacrificing, concerned for others, not as powerful, not famous, average people. This group more easily trusts God and gives to others.

These people, because of their dependence on and trust in God and concern for others, will be first in God's kingdom.

"Many who are first will be last, and many who are last will be first."
Matthew 19:30

Living It

Margot wants to be important. She pushes unimportant girls out of her way. She pays no attention to anyone she feels can't do something for her. Margot is all about Margot. She thinks she's first, but she's really last in line from Jesus' viewpoint.

Nathalie, on the other hand, cares a lot for other people. She seeks out girls who are by themselves and tries to include them in conversation. She gives her time to help in soup kitchens. Nathalie is on the road to being first, but that doesn't really matter to her. It isn't why she does what she does.

Bigger Faith

> "Truly I tell you, if you have faith and do not doubt, not only can you do what was done to the fig tree, but also you can say to this mountain, 'Go, throw yourself into the sea,' and it will be done."
>
> Matthew 21:21

Jesus had just declared that a particular fig tree would never grow fruit again and He told His followers that if they just had enough faith they could do that or even make a mountain fall into the sea.

The power of Jesus is available to His followers. You can move mountains if you just have enough faith.

How does a girl learn to have faith that big? Practice, trust, depend, believe.

Living It

Becca loves God and she would love to be able to make a difference in the world for Him. "If I had power like Jesus, I would use it to help people with problems and to help others come to know Him." Becca could do that, too.

She starts small by trusting God with small things, like helping her to get over having nightmares. Every time Becca sees God answer a prayer, protect her or help her, her faith grows. It's a journey to learn and grow in faith.

Be Careful How You Live

Watch out for teachers who do not practice what they preach.

Jesus warns you to make sure that the teachers you listen to live in ways that match what they teach.

Some people like to tell others what to do but they won't do a single thing to help make sure the work gets done. These types of people have way too much pride.

> "Do everything they tell you. But do not do what they do, for they do not practice what they preach. They tie up heavy, cumbersome loads and put them on other people's shoulders, but they themselves are not willing to lift a finger to move them."
>
> Matthew 23:3-4

Living It

It is a big responsibility to be a teacher who tries to help people understand how to know God and live for Him.

Teachers who tell others how to live for God but whose own lives don't match those guidelines will answer to God for their hypocrisy.

Be careful which teachers you follow and be careful how you live. Don't say one thing but then live in a different way.

Show-Offs

> "Everything they do is done for people to see."
>
> Matthew 23:5

Jesus is speaking here about religious leaders who make a big show of being religious.

They do showy religious things but make sure that others are watching. They want other people to notice how religious they are and think they are super important. They want places of honor and for people to treat them as though they are really important.

All they do is for their own sake, not for God at all.

Living It

Lucy is pretty impressed with herself. She wants other girls to think she is important and influential. Sometimes she does things that make it look like she really cares about the other girls, but she really doesn't.

Everything Lucy does is for show and not for God or for others. Lucy will answer to God for this behavior. It's contrary to everything Jesus teaches.

One Father

God is the supreme authority in the world and He won't share that with anyone or anything else. God desires respect and worship and love greater than that which is given to any earthly person.

Of course, this statement does not mean that you do not call your parent father or dad. It simply means that no human should ever be on equal footing with God.

> "Do not call anyone on earth 'father,' for you have one Father, and He is in heaven."
>
> Matthew 23:9

Living It

Lisa is a Daddy's girl. She thinks her dad can fix anything and do anything. She thinks he is the smartest man in the whole wide world!

One thing Lisa's dad does that is super smart is that he reminds Lisa that while he is her dad and he loves her a lot, God is her Father and He deserves the most adoration and praise!

False Teachers

"Watch out that no one deceives you."
Matthew 24:4

Sadly, there are those who try to get people to follow them instead of Jesus. They create their own religions (often called cults) but they pretend to be teaching people about Jesus.

Jesus warns His followers to be careful about the teachers they listen to by testing what they teach against the Bible and making sure that they match.

If you ever have questions about a teacher, ask God to direct you and talk to someone you respect for advice.

Living It

Penelope's sister has always been a strong Christian, but since she went away to college she has gotten kind of weird. She became involved with a group near her school that just seems a little off-center from what Penelope and her parents believe.

Penelope is afraid that her sister has been deceived by a false teacher. She prays for wisdom and for her sister's eyes to be opened.

Be Ready

Jesus is God's Son, but some things God has not even told Jesus – for example, the time when Jesus comes back to earth to take His followers to heaven.

If Jesus doesn't know – and He says that only God knows – then it makes sense that no human knows when that day will come.

People who claim to be able to predict the day when Jesus will return are mistaken and should not be listened to.

> "About that day or hour no one knows, not even the angels in heaven, nor the Son, but only the Father."
> Matthew 24:36

Living It

Jamie knows that Jesus will come back one day to take His followers to heaven. She's heard people say that they know when that will happen. So far they've all been wrong.

Jamie knows that she should just be ready to go with Him whenever He does come. Jamie reads her Bible and tries to obey its teachings. She prays and stays close to Jesus. Jamie can't wait to see Him face to face!

Future Rewards

"Then the King will say to those on His right, 'Come, you who are blessed by My Father; take your inheritance, the kingdom prepared for you since the creation of the world.'"

Matthew 25:34

This is a beautiful promise from Jesus. He will come back to earth one day to gather His followers and take them to heaven.

Jesus promises that His followers will receive the rewards and promises of eternal life with Him.

The kingdom of heaven has been prepared for all believers since the beginning of time. It is a beautiful place to spend forever with Jesus!

Living It

Following Jesus is not always easy. You may have problems because you have chosen to accept Him. He will walk with you every step of the way and teach you how to follow Him.

Jesus promises that not only will He be with you every day of your life, He is preparing a special place for you to be with Him in heaven ... forever!

Caring for Others

Jesus always emphasized caring for others. An important part of living for Him is taking care of others, especially those who are poor and lonely.

People who are undesirable and need a lot of help are the ones Jesus wants you to reach out to. By helping them, you show your love for Jesus.

> "I was hungry and you gave Me something to eat, I was thirsty and you gave Me something to drink, I was a stranger and you invited Me in, I needed clothes and you clothed Me, I was sick and you looked after Me, I was in prison and you came to visit Me."
>
> Matthew 25:35-36

Living It

Donating to a food pantry, serving meals to homeless people, collecting clothing for the poor, visiting the sick, running errands, visiting prison inmates or their families, all of these are ways in which a girl can put Jesus' teaching into practice.

There are so many things a girl can do to help others and share Jesus' love. Just look around and see how you can get involved.

Serving Jesus

"The King will reply,
'Truly I tell you,
whatever you did
for one of the least
of these brothers
and sisters of Mine,
you did for Me.'"

Matthew 25:40

Jesus had just listed several wonderful things that people had done – feeding the hungry, clothing the naked, caring for the sick and visiting those in prison.

Now He says that when they did those kind things for others, they were really serving Him.

Jesus emphasizes over and over how important it is to care for others and now He says that caring for others is actually showing your love for Him!

Living It

How can helping other people be the same as helping Jesus? Remember that Jesus said it is easy to be kind to your friends – anyone can do that.

So, when you go out of your comfort zone and help people who you don't know or who may be a bit less desirable, you are showing your love for Jesus.

A Fresh Start

The teachings of Jesus were different from what people had heard before. His teachings were pretty much the opposite of what the religious leaders taught.

So, Jesus said that it wouldn't work to take His new teachings and try to wrap them into your current way of life.

Following Jesus means starting fresh ... with Him.

"No one sews a patch of unshrunk cloth on an old garment. Otherwise, the new piece will pull away from the old, making the tear worse."

Mark 2:21

Living It

Kaylie wants to follow Jesus ... kind of. What she tries to do is to keep living her life the way she always has – with all her old habits and old friends, but just add Jesus in. Yeah, it doesn't work.

Kaylie soon finds that trying to include Jesus in her current life just causes problems with her and her friends. She needs to let Jesus take over her whole life so she can have a fresh start with Him at the center of her life.

Be More Forgiving

"With the measure you use, it will be measured to you – and even more."

Mark 4:24

What kind of measuring stick do you use to judge other people? Is it a short stick that does not give them much room to make mistakes or disappoint you?

Did you know that the way you judge other people is the way you will be judged? Does that make you want to be a little more forgiving and understanding of others? Good.

Living It

Terra complains a lot that her friend Anna is so critical. "She makes fun of my hair or another girl's clothes. She complains about absolutely everything! I can't stand it!"

What Terra doesn't realize is that her friends feel the same way about her. They think she is just as critical as Anna. Terra needs to be careful about how she judges her friend – her friends will judge her the same way.

November

Don't Be Afraid

> "Why are you so afraid? Do you still have no faith?"
>
> Mark 4:40

Jesus asked His disciples this after He had calmed a storm on the sea. He had just performed an amazing miracle – the weather did what He told it to!

They had, however, seen Him do other miracles before. They had traveled with Him and heard all His teachings, but they still didn't trust Him enough to stop being afraid.

Jesus must have wondered what else He had to do or say to get them to trust Him completely!

Living It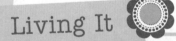

Paula prayed for help in making friends. That prayer was answered. She prayed for her grandfather who was very sick and he did get better. It would seem that Paula's faith would grow stronger each time she saw God answer a prayer.

But fear sometimes gripped Paula's heart. It is taking a long time for her to trust Jesus enough to not be afraid, but she is getting there.

My Way or the Highway

Jesus has a way with words, doesn't He? He almost seems to be giving a compliment to people who make up their own rules as to how to live the Christian life, but He isn't.

They might twist God's commands just a bit to fit their own rules or they may totally toss God's commands in the garbage. Either way it's wrong. They are not truly obeying God and they will answer to Him for their selfishness.

> "You have a fine way of setting aside the commands of God in order to observe your own traditions!"
>
> Mark 7:9

Living It

"God didn't really mean that talking about our friends is gossip," Nella firmly informed her friend Angie. "I mean, seriously. He didn't really know what life was going to be like when the world got this crowded and this busy. I'm sure it's not gossip to talk about what someone else does."

Wrong. Nella is definitely putting a twist on God's commands. Gossip was wrong in Jesus' day and it is wrong today. Pay attention to God's commands and obey them.

Dirty on the Inside

"For it is from within, out of a person's heart, that evil thoughts come, sexual immorality, theft, murder, adultery, greed, malice, deceit, lewdness, envy, slander, arrogance and folly. All these evils come from inside and defile a person.'"

Mark 7:21-23

Sin starts on the inside because, the truth is, you make a decision in your heart to disobey. It's your choice.

You can walk away from a tempting situation, or you can stick around and let the temptation take hold in your heart. Once that happens ... you're going to do it and that is what makes you unclean in God's sight.

Living It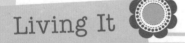

Tina knows the difference between right and wrong. Her parents have taught her that all her life. But when she started hanging around with some girls who didn't care about Jesus, some of their bad habits began rubbing off on her.

One of those habits was how she used God's name as a joke or even a swear word. She knew better, but she wanted to fit in with her friends so she made the choice to speak as they did. Misusing God's name is a sin. She chose it. She did it.

Practical Compassion

Jesus is so practical. He knew that the thousands of people around Him that day had come to hear Him teach and to see Him do miracles.

Jesus also knew that they needed food. They couldn't really listen to Him teach if they were hungry. Jesus wanted their physical needs met as well as their spiritual needs. Pretty cool, eh?

If He did that for them, He will do it for you, too.

> "I have compassion for these people; they have already been with Me three days and have nothing to eat."
>
> Mark 8:2

Living It

Of course, Jesus may also want you to be a part of the solution to meeting physical needs for others. If your needs are all met – you have a home, clothes and food – then look around your town, county, state, world. You will find people who don't have all that you do. How can you help? What can you do? Collect food for a homeless shelter? Give money to organizations that supply food? Whatever Jesus plants in your heart, He will help you do because He cares about physical needs as well as spiritual needs.

Who Do You Say He Is?

"Who do people say I am? But what about you?" He asked. "Who do you say I am?"

Mark 8:27, 29

Jesus asked Peter, one of His closest followers what the word on the street was about Him.

He had done all kinds of miracles in God's name. He had taught about God and how to live for Him, so He wondered if people were getting it. Had they begun to believe that He was God's Son, the Messiah, who had come to save the world?

A couple of verses later Jesus asked Peter, "OK, who do you say I am?" Peter was one of Jesus' closest friends – did he get it?

Living It

Chloe knows who Jesus is. At least she thinks she does. Her parents have taught her that He is the Son of God who died for her sins and rose back to life. They taught that He is her Savior and will come one day to take all His children to heaven.

Yes, that's what they taught Chloe. But she doesn't read her Bible, doesn't pray, doesn't think about Jesus at all most days. So, while her head may know who He is, her heart says He is no one special. What does your heart say? Who is Jesus to you?

Follow Jesus

What was Jesus talking about? What does it mean to deny yourself?

The Christian life is one of surrender. Denying yourself means surrendering your will and desires to whatever Christ wants for you.

Taking up your cross means being willing to serve Christ in the way He leads you when life gets tough or when you don't want to do stuff or even when you're tired. Follow Him. You'll never regret it.

> "Whoever wants to be My disciple must deny themselves and take up their cross and follow Me."
> Mark 8:34

Living It

Ariana didn't get what Jesus was saying until she had a chance for a weekly babysitting job while the child's parents played golf. She was saving up for an awesome pair of jeans that cost so much her parents said she had to pay for them herself.

She was taking every job she could get. But, this job was every Sunday morning. That meant no church. Should she take it for the money? It paid really well! Or, should she choose church? Denying her own wants and taking up her cross, in this situation, meant turning down the weekly job.

Finding Life

> "Whoever wants to save their life will lose it, but whoever loses their life for Me and for the gospel will save it."
>
> Mark 8:35

Some people feel that to give up control over their own lives means they are losing their lives. Because they have lost control it may feel as though they are free falling in space. It's scary.

But when you give up control to Jesus then you are really saving your life. You are turning from sin and from the hopelessness of a life without Him, that has no hope of heaven.

Giving your life to Jesus actually gives you purpose and direction.

Living It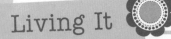

Beatrice has control issues. She knows it, too. She likes to be in charge by telling her friends what they should do, how they should think and what they should say. Her room has everything in its place and she knows what her plan is for each day.

So, giving up control of her life to Jesus did not happen easily. She fought it, in fact. She even tried to tell Him what to do. Yeah, that didn't work so well. Once Beatrice surrendered control, though, she found her life more purposeful every day. She didn't lose her life. She found it!

Caring for All

During Jesus' time on earth children, women, the sick and the poor were considered unimportant by powerful people and even by religious leaders. Healthy, wealthy men were the important ones. But not to Jesus.

When Jesus saw some children He took the opportunity to point out that people who cared about them were actually caring about Him and His Father.

Jesus cared about those who were unimportant to others and He wanted His followers to do the same.

> "Whoever welcomes one of these little children in My name welcomes Me; and whoever welcomes Me does not welcome Me but the One who sent Me."
>
> ❋ Mark 9:37

Living It

"It must be hard to be the new girl in school," thought Alison. She had noticed a new girl who was always alone. "She must be pretty lonely," Alison decided. None of the other girls wanted to talk to the new girl.

Alison remembered that Jesus said to care about all people, so she asked the new girl to sit with her at lunchtime and they talked some. It felt good to be nice to someone who was ignored by others.

Number One?

> "Truly I tell you, anyone who will not receive the kingdom of God like a little child will never enter it."
>
> Mark 10:15

Maybe you've heard the old saying, "she toots her own horn." It means that a girl who is full of pride makes sure everyone knows how important and special she is.

Jesus isn't impressed with a person who is impressed with herself. To be great in God's kingdom, one must be humble and filled with trust in Him.

Living It

If you asked Dawn if she had a problem with pride, she would say no. But when her friends think about it, they realize that she talks about herself all the time. She always has to be the center of attention. She usually has a story that is better than anyone else's. Dawn is not humble and she doesn't trust God completely because she feels that she can handle anything that happens by herself. After all, she is Dawn! Yeah, Dawn needs to learn that humility, faith, trust and love are more important than always being Number One herself.

Keeping the Commandments

A rich man asked Jesus how to be sure of eternal life. Jesus first focused the man's thoughts on how he treated others. Was he kind? Was he fair? Was he moral? Did he treat others with the respect and honor they deserved?

It matters to Jesus how people treat one another. Love for God is shown not just by how you treat Him, but also by how you treat others.

"You know the commandments: 'You shall not murder, you shall not commit adultery, you shall not steal, you shall not give false testimony, you shall not defraud, honor your father and mother.'"

Mark 10:19

Living It

Laura knows the commandments Jesus is speaking of here. She figures she is pretty good at keeping them, except maybe for the one on false testimony.

Does she sometimes bend the truth a little? Yes. Does she join in conversation that would be considered gossip about other girls? Yes. Does she even stretch the truth when talking about someone else just to make her story good or make herself look better? Yes. Maybe Laura needs to reconsider how well she is obeying the commandments.

Go For It!

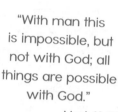

"With man this is impossible, but not with God; all things are possible with God."

Mark 10:27

How amazing is this statement? **Nothing** is impossible for God.

Jesus made this statement in response to His disciples' question about how hard it is for a rich person to be saved. His response is wonderful because it reminds you that none of your problems are too big for Him. You can be sure that He can handle any prayer request you have.

Never give up on God – He can do anything!

Living It

Keshia used to pray a lot. She faithfully supported her friends and family in prayer. But now she has something to pray about that is really big. It's so big that she isn't sure even God can handle it. Her grandpa is really sick. He might even die.

Keshia knows she should pray for him, but she isn't sure God can make him well. Actually, she wasn't sure until she read this verse. Now she knows she can pray for Grandpa and anything else, because nothing is impossible with God!

Give All to Jesus

Jesus wants 100% of you – the girl who surrenders completely to Him will never be sorry. Jesus promises that!

When He says you will get back 100 times what you give Him, is He talking about money? No. Money doesn't really matter to Jesus. He's talking about the blessings of knowing and serving Him – peace, joy, assurance that you are loved, purpose in your life, answered prayers and the promise of eternal life.

These blessings are too great to even count.

> "No one who has left home or brothers or sisters or mother or father or children or fields for Me and the gospel will fail to receive a hundred times as much in this present age: homes, brothers, sisters, mothers, children and fields – along with persecutions – and in the age to come, eternal life."
>
> ✳ Mark 10:29-30

Living It

Addison doesn't get what Jesus means about leaving your family and your work to follow Him. She wonders if He is saying that the only people who will be blessed are those who go to other countries as missionaries.

No, He's just saying that nothing should be more important than serving Him. In order for that to happen, Addison has to trust Him enough to give up control of her life and believe that He will take complete care of her.

God's Word

"Heaven and earth will pass away, but My words will never pass away."

Mark 13:31

God's Word is a gift to you. The Bible is God's message to you. It contains much of what He wants you to know about Him and His care for you. He is pleased when you read it because you get to know Him better through doing so.

God's Word has survived through the centuries even though people have tried to destroy it. Jesus says that it will never be lost. No matter what else happens, God's Word will survive.

Living It

Bethany's favorite thing in the whole world is to talk with her friends. They can talk for hours; sharing their dreams and their problems, and just getting to know each other better.

Reading God's Word is like having a conversation with God. The more Bethany reads God's Word the better she knows Him and the more she understands about Him. Bethany is very thankful for the Bible.

Worship Matters

Think about this woman. She was a nobody in the eyes of the men around Jesus.

Women weren't considered very important in that time. She worshiped Jesus by pouring expensive perfume on Him. The men there criticized her for that, but Jesus knew she was worshiping Him.

What she did was so important that it was recorded in the Bible and people are still talking about her thousands of years later. Worship matters.

> "Truly I tell you, wherever the gospel is preached throughout the world, what she has done will also be told, in memory of her."
>
> Mark 14:9

Living It

Worship happens in different ways for different people. Kayla worships through music – singing it and listening to it. Mallory worships through words – reading and writing. Christy worships through art – painting and observing.

Worship is a very personal experience and comes from a heart surrendered to God and focused on honoring and praising Him.

He's Coming Back

"I am," said Jesus. "And you will see the Son of Man sitting at the right hand of the Mighty One and coming on the clouds of heaven."

Mark 14:62

A religious leader asked Jesus point-blank if He was the Messiah. Jesus' answer was, "I am." Jesus knew that the man asking Him the question was not a friend but Jesus pointedly answered that He is indeed God's Son, the Messiah.

And not only that, He promised that He would one day come back to earth as a judge of the sins of mankind.

Living It

Often when Jesus talked about coming back to take His followers to heaven, He was speaking to His friends and He spoke with a hopeful promise.

This time, He seems to speak more firmly and the idea of judgment comes through. Perhaps He was trying to get His listeners to take Him seriously and get their lives in order by obeying and serving Him. He will come back. Be ready.

One Way

The pathway to salvation and being with Jesus forever in heaven is a personal one. Each girl must make her own choice about believing.

You can't count on salvation just because your parents or friends are saved. There is only one way to salvation – believe.

The person who does not believe is not saved and will not go to heaven.

"Whoever believes and is baptized will be saved, but whoever does not believe will be condemned."

Mark 16:16

Living It

Accepting Jesus as Savior is a big decision to Kelsie. She doesn't see the necessity of it. Her mom and dad are strong Christians so she's pretty sure she will go to heaven with them. After all, they take her everywhere.

Well, not this time, Kelsie. She must make her own decision to believe in Jesus and accept Him as Savior. That's the only way!

Focus on Jesus

> "It is written: 'Man shall not live on bread alone.'"
>
> Luke 4:4

Satan tempted Jesus to try to get Him to turn away from God and honor Satan.

Jesus didn't do it, of course. But you learn some interesting things during this experience. One is to stop thinking about yourself, whether you're hungry, cold, poor, rich, or whatever.

Don't focus on your physical needs. Instead, focus on Jesus and His care for you.

Living It

Janna's dad lost his job and the family has been cutting corners just to make ends meet. Sometimes Janna has to go to bed hungry. It's hard to think about anything else when she is hungry.

Janna could focus all her energy on that, but this verse tells her not to do that. Even as she's hungry, she can remember that God supplies her needs.

Humble Hearts

You don't have to be financially poor to be a part of God's kingdom. You just need to be humble and dependent on God.

That is sometimes a difficult thing for wealthy and powerful people. They may be used to being in charge rather than surrendered to someone else's will.

Jesus lived an example of this humility – serving others, helping people who others ignored and by doing what God wanted Him to.

> "Blessed are you who are poor, for yours is the kingdom of God."
> Luke 6:20

Living It

Macie is the kind of girl who no one notices. She seems to be invisible. Others walk by her, chatting and giggling and do not even look at her. She has decided that it is hard to make friends if you don't have friends. Everyone seems to think there is something wrong with her or she would already have friends. But Patti does notice Macie. One lunchtime, Patti left her group of friends and went over to sit by Macie. Some of her friends made fun of her, but she didn't care. Patti felt that she was doing what Jesus would do if He were in her school.

Good Hunger

"Blessed are you who hunger now, for you will be satisfied."

Luke 6:21

What do you hunger for? What do you want more and more and more of? Time with friends? Popularity? Playing sport? Knowledge? Knowing God better?

Jesus said that if you hunger for the right things you will be satisfied. Wanting to know God better, serve Him more fully, be more obedient to Him ... that's what will make you feel satisfied and fulfilled.

Living It

When Raegan asked Jesus into her heart she knew that she loved Him. She has been reading her Bible and getting to know Him better and that has helped her love Him more.

Raegan doesn't understand everything she reads in His Word, but she asks her parents or Sunday school teacher to explain things. The more she reads, the more she wants to read. Raegan can't get enough of learning about Him and His love for her!

Blessed Obedience

Some people will not like you just because you follow Jesus.

Your obedience to God will make them uncomfortable and they may show that by making fun of you, shutting you out of their group of friends and just generally insulting you.

Jesus reminds you that it's OK. You will be blessed for your obedience by Him!

"Blessed are you when people hate you, when they exclude you and insult you and reject your name as evil, because of the Son of Man."

Luke 6:22

Living It

Laura is running for class president. Her opponent, Melissa, does not fight fair. She knows that Laura is a Christian and tries to live her life in obedience to God. So Melissa starts a "whisper campaign" about that.

She drops little comments to someone about Laura being a religious freak, no fun because her head is always in the Bible, doesn't ever have any fun ... things like that. Laura is being insulted just because she follows God. He will bless her for her obedience, you can be sure of that.

Serve God or Money

"Woe to you who are rich, for you have already received your comfort."

Luke 6:24

Money. Some people never have enough. The more they have, the more they want.

Sure, they share some of their money. The sad thing is that all their focus is on getting more and then on investing their money and protecting it. Life becomes all about money. It's sad because this person doesn't make serving, loving and obeying God her focus but thinks more about money than Him.

Well, the money is all she's going to have in the long run, not God.

Living It

Lainie has a great example of the opposite of this statement. Her mom and dad both work hard at their jobs and they earn enough money to make life comfortable for the family. But, money isn't their goal. They make sure there is time to spend together as a family. They also spend time with other family and friends. They generously give money to help others and they spend time helping others. Lainie goes with them sometimes to work in the food pantry and other things they do. Their focus is on serving God, not money.

So, is Jesus saying that it is better for you to be hungry and sad?

No, He isn't saying that. Jesus hopes you will notice when others do not have enough food or need help and He wants His followers to do the helping. If a girl thinks only about herself and her needs and having fun, then woe to her.

But, if she helps others who do not have enough of what they need, then she is being Jesus to them. No more woes.

> "Woe to you who are well fed now, for you will go hungry. Woe to you who laugh now, for you will mourn and weep."
>
> Luke 6:25

Living It

Some girls think, "I'm just a kid, what can I do to help someone who doesn't have enough food?" Some girls would think that, then forget about it and get themselves a snack, but not Talia.

She heard that the food pantry was short on peanut butter. So, she started collecting jars of peanut butter. She made flyers to put up around town. She went door to door collecting donations. Then, when she had jars and jars of peanut butter to donate, she had a party doing it!

A Good Student

> "The student is not above the teacher, but everyone who is fully trained will be like their teacher."
>
> Luke 6:40

Some girls are hard to teach because they think they know everything already.

When the teacher tries to explain a lesson, these girls won't listen. After all, they know the answers better than the teacher.

Jesus reminds you that you do not know more than He does. Only by having an open mind and heart, can you learn to be like Him.

Living It

Wendi takes piano lessons. She doesn't like doing the exercises that are necessary to being a good musician. When her teacher assigns exercises, Wendi argues that she doesn't need to do them. This is a classic example of the student thinking she knows more than her teacher. She will only learn to be a better pianist if she accepts training from her teacher. In the same way, you will only learn to be a better Christian by accepting training from Jesus. Understand that you do not know more than your teacher, and have an open spirit to learn from Him.

Good Comes from Good

It's hopeless to expect good to come from bad.

If you try to make a fancy dinner using weeds and dirt, you'll be disappointed. If you expect good and kind behavior from a heart that cares nothing about God or others, you will also be disappointed.

Jesus' example of a tree having fruit of a certain kind shows that He knows a heart that is devoted to Him shows love and kindness to others.

A heart that doesn't know God cannot be expected to show love and concern for others.

> "Each tree is recognized by its own fruit. People do not pick figs from thornbushes, or grapes from briers."
>
> Luke 6:44

Living It

One of Cici's friends is not a Christian and makes it very clear that she doesn't want to be told anything about God. But when she has a crisis in her life, who does she go to for sympathy and advice? Yes, Cici.

Because she has seen how Cici treats others, she knows that she will receive love and compassion from Cici. She has seen the fruit of Cici's life.

The Firmest Foundation

"I will show you what it's like when someone comes to Me, listens to my teaching, and then follows it. It is like a person building a house who digs deep and lays the foundation on solid rock. When the floodwaters rise and break against that house, it stands firm because it is well built."

Luke 6:47-48 NLT

Sometimes people take the easy way out of problems.

Jesus compares this laziness to the example of a house built on a good foundation – even the worst storm cannot shake it because its foundation is firm.

How does a girl build a firm foundation for life? By spending time reading God's Word, praying and building a strong relationship of trust with Jesus. Then, whatever happens in your life, your foundation will be firm.

Living It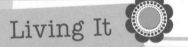

Quin doesn't spend time with God every day. Once in a while she reads her Bible and prays when there is something she wants. Maybe Quin doesn't think this is a big deal, but the truth is that she is not building the good foundation of a strong relationship with Jesus.

When she needs that foundation to hold her up during tough times she will crumble. But, there's still time to fix it – spend time with Jesus every day!

No Hopelessness

The woman Jesus spoke these words to could have felt hopeless.

She had two strikes against her – she was known to live a sinful life and she was a woman, which, in those days, was a disadvantage.

She had two bad things to overcome. Still, she courageously came to Jesus when He was surrounded by a group of men and worshiped Him.

Jesus probably knew her reputation of a sinful lifestyle, but He could also see her heart. He saw that she had faith in Him. That faith saved her and promised a life of peace.

"Your faith has saved you; go in peace."
Luke 7:50

Living It

Most of the time Rhoda feels pretty good, but once in a while she feels a little hopeless. That hopelessness comes when she stops trusting Jesus and starts thinking about problems or fears she has.

Staying close to Jesus and keeping her faith and trust in Him strong is what gives her hope and peace. He's never let her down and she is pretty sure that He won't start any time soon!

Necessary Faith

> "The knowledge of the secrets of the kingdom of God has been given to you, but to others I speak in parables, so that, 'though seeing, they may not see; though hearing, they may not understand.'"
>
> Luke 8:10

Over and over again Jesus stresses how important faith is.

If you don't believe Jesus is God's Son and that He came to earth to teach about the best way to know God and that He was killed and rose back to life, then the true message of His teaching will make no sense to you.

It will be like hearing someone speak a language you don't understand. Jesus' message is for His followers.

Living It

Mariah and her family visited Italy. She learned a few Italian words and phrases before the trip, but not enough to have a conversation. So, when someone spoke to her, all she could do was nod her head and smile. She didn't understand a word.

That's how the message of Scripture sounds to people who don't believe in Jesus. They can understand the basic message (which hopefully leads them to salvation), but the deeper lessons – the ones that would help them grow mature – make no sense to them. Start with the basics, then grow.

Light in the Darkness

What good is a light that is hidden? The purpose of light is to break through darkness and reveal what is hidden by that darkness.

Jesus called Himself the Light of the World and when a girl asks Jesus to be her Savior, His light comes into her life. She becomes one more point of light in a world filled with the darkness of sin.

> "No one lights a lamp and hides it in a clay jar or puts it under a bed. Instead, they put it on a stand, so that those who come in can see the light."
>
> Luke 8:16

Living It

Lydia is the first person in her whole family to become a Christian. She is able to be a light for Jesus to her family. How does she do that?

By showing patience, love and unselfishness, and by being concerned about her family members. She gives the credit for all this kindness to Jesus, because it is by His power that she has changed from how she once behaved.

No Secrets

> "There is nothing hidden that will not be disclosed, and nothing concealed that will not be known or brought out into the open."
>
> Luke 8:17

Secrets are fun sometimes.

Secrets that are about surprises and happy things are fun. But, secrets that you are trying to keep someone from knowing; maybe about something wrong you've done, are not good.

Here's an interesting thing about secrets – you can't keep them from God. He knows and sees everything.

Everything will be revealed to Him eventually and you will have to answer to Him for the choices you have made.

Living It

Charlie thinks she is pretty smart. She thinks that the things she thinks but doesn't say out loud and the things she reads or watches on the computer when she is alone are secrets and that no one knows about them.

She's wrong. Jesus knows her thoughts and He sees her actions, and one day she will answer to Him for those things. There are no secrets from God.

Good Listening

What kind of listener are you? Do you hear the first couple of words, then shut your ears because you think you know what the rest of a sentence is? Do you listen with your mind already made up?

Listening with an open mind and heart is the best way to learn. If you listen with your mind made up already, thinking that you know everything, you will not learn very much.

> "Consider carefully how you listen. Whoever has will be given more; whoever does not have, even what they think they have will be taken from them."
>
> Luke 8:18

Living It

Charlotte is annoying to talk with. She can't wait for anyone to finish a sentence, she finishes it herself. She's not always right either. Her friends have pretty much stopped talking to her because she doesn't listen anyway.

Charlotte does the same thing with God. She thinks she has all the answers so there's no reason to listen to His Word or to be quiet before Him and listen for His voice to guide her. Charlotte is not learning more about God by behaving this way. She must listen to Him and have a heart that is open to learning.

December

The Least of All

"Whoever welcomes this little child in My name welcomes Me; and whoever welcomes Me welcomes the One who sent Me. For it is the one who is least among you all who is the greatest."

Luke 9:48

People who think they are important or powerful often associate only with other important or powerful people. They think that they are too important to have anything to do with those who are not as important as they are.

These people really miss the point of Jesus' teaching. Power and importance are nothing to Him. Humility, love for others, devotion to Jesus ... those are what make you great.

Living It

What does this teaching mean to someone your age? Think about it – are you friendly to those who aren't as popular as you? Are you kind to those who aren't kind to you? Do you take time to talk with younger girls and be an example to them of a kind, loving person?

Jesus always pointed out that kindness and concern for others is very important in living for Him.

Be Still

It's good to be busy. Martha was super-busy preparing dinner. But she was not only busy, she was annoyed that her sister wasn't helping her. Mary was just sitting beside Jesus and listening to what He said.

Martha thought that Jesus should make Mary help her, but Jesus was pleased that Mary wanted to spend time with Him. That's the most important thing – spend time with Jesus and get to know Him.

"Martha, Martha," the Lord answered, "you are worried and upset about many things, but few things are needed – or indeed only one. Mary has chosen what is better, and it will not be taken away from her."

Luke 10:41-42

Living It

Amanda is a "take-charge" girl. If you want something done, put Amanda in charge and it will be taken care of. The struggle Amanda has is to keep the balance in her life between being busy, but also being still before Jesus.

Really being quiet ... not talking, reading, watching TV or anything, just being quiet and hearing what He wants to say to her.

Opportunity Unlimited

> "So I say to you: Ask and it will be given to you; seek and you will find; knock and the door will be opened to you."
>
> Luke 11:9

Jesus had just taught His followers the Lord's Prayer. He added this statement, which is a promise that God hears your prayers. He loves you and wants to give you good gifts.

But don't think God is a big "Santa Claus" who will give you absolutely anything you want. It doesn't work that way. Ask, seek and knock as you spend time in His Word and prayer. Then your requests will be guided and directed by His Spirit.

Living It

Prayer is an amazing gift. Think about it ... you have the listening ear of the Creator of all things; the most powerful one in the universe.

What do you do with that opportunity? Do you pray, seek and ask? Do you believe He will answer? Do you trust His answers? Pray with confidence and trust the results.

Just Ask

Way back in the Old Testament, the Holy Spirit was promised to God's people one day. The Spirit is an amazing gift to people. He lives in your heart so that God's guidance is always with you.

Jesus considers the Holy Spirit to be a very special gift and one that is given because of true love by God for His children.

> "If you then, though you are evil, know how to give good gifts to your children, how much more will your Father in heaven give the Holy Spirit to those who ask Him!"
>
> Luke 11:13

Living It

Ask for the Spirit. Does it seem strange to you that you have to ask for the Holy Spirit? Well, since you have to ask, you must think about it. And having the Spirit in your life becomes your choice ... something you want. Perhaps then you won't take it lightly.

The gift of the Spirit is evidence of the pure love the Father has for you. He wants to give you wonderful, amazing things because He loves you so much. The Spirit is the best of all gifts. Receive Him and call on Him daily for guidance.

Hearing Isn't Enough

"Blessed rather are those who hear the Word of God and obey it."

Luke 11:28

A woman in the crowd had just called out, "Blessed is Your mother who gave You birth!" and Jesus' response is the Scripture verse for today.

Not only hearing God's Word is important, but also obeying it is what gives blessings. Jesus wasn't dismissing His earthly mother as unimportant, but He was emphasizing how very important it is to obey His Word.

Living It

Kaiya has heard God's Word her whole life. Her parents have family devotions with the kids and take them to church and Sunday school. So Kaiya has heard all the Bible stories and memorized all the Scripture verses to get her badges.

But just hearing the Word doesn't do much good. It's when Kaiya understands it and obeys it that she is blessed. She is living for Jesus when she obeys it.

Give to the Poor

This is the end of a story Jesus told about a rich man who had so many crops that he didn't know what to do. Instead of sharing what he had with those who didn't have much food, he just built a bigger barn to store all he had.

He thought he was set for life. But His life would end that very night and he would learn that he had not pleased God by thinking only of himself instead of how he could help others.

> "God said to him, 'You fool! This very night your life will be demanded from you. Then who will get what you have prepared for yourself?' This is how it will be with whoever stores up things for themselves but is not rich toward God."
>
> Luke 12:20-21

Living It

Over and over and over Jesus said not to worry about money. He said to use what you need, then give to the poor. He said to care about others more than you care about yourself. Fran gets it and so do her parents. Her parents are generous to organizations that help poor people around the world.

They've taught Fran to share a part of her allowance, too. They give of their money and their time to help in any way they can. They are storing up treasures in heaven.

Trusting God

> "Therefore I tell you, do not worry about your life, what you will eat; or about your body, what you will wear. Life is more than food, and the body more than clothes."
>
> Luke 12:22-23

Worry may be the biggest enemy for a Christian. It's hard not to worry, but the truth is that worry and trust cannot live in your heart at the same time.

If you trust God to take care of you and give you what you need, then you won't need to worry about those things. If you don't trust Him; well, that's where worry comes in. You must learn that you can trust God to take care of you.

Living It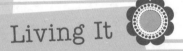

Paula's family is moving across the country. She's going to leave her friends, grandparents, school, church and home. Everything will be new and Paula is scared. OK, she's not worried about food, but she does kind of wonder what style of clothes the girls in her new school wear. She's worried that she won't be able to make friends. She's worried about being lonely.

If Paula would trust God with these things ... tell Him what she's afraid of and let Him take care of them, then she wouldn't have to be so worried. It's not easy, but she'll be so glad she did!

World-Class Worry

You can worry non-stop about how long you're going to live, but you can't do anything about it. You can't do a thing to change it. So – why worry?

Jesus wants you to know that you can trust Him. He loves you more than you can imagine. So trust God to take complete care of you, every moment of every day that He gives you.

> "Who of you by worrying can add a single hour to your life? Since you cannot do this very little thing, why do you worry about the rest?"
>
> Luke 12:25-26

Living It

Wanda is a world-class worrier. She worries about earthquakes and storms. She worries that her friends will get mad at her. She worries that her dad will lose his job. She worries that she will get sick. Seriously, she worries about everything, mostly about things that she can't do anything about or things that are not really that serious.

Wanda the Worrier must learn to be Wanda the Truster as she begins to trust Jesus to take care of everything.

Misplaced Treasure

> "Where your treasure is, there your heart will be also."
>
> Luke 12:34

Some people try to divide their hearts. They think it's possible to put all their energy, thoughts and time into one thing, but then say that their hearts belong totally to God.

It doesn't work. The reality is that your treasure becomes whatever occupies your time, thoughts and energy and if it isn't knowing and serving God, then your treasure is in the wrong place.

Living It

Carol tries to have it all. She has a real gift for playing the violin and she loves it. She practices for hours. She listens to violin recordings when she isn't practicing. Carol's life and thoughts are consumed with improving her ability. Carol also says that her heart is devoted to God. It's fine that Carol is a good violin player who wants to improve her skill ... after all, God gave her the gift. Here's the problem: When anything occupies your time and thoughts so much that you don't have time to read the Bible or talk with God ... then your treasure is in the wrong place.

Pride Comes Before a Fall

Do you think you are someone special? Someone who is better than those around you? Do you need to be Number One, the center of attention, the life of the party? Well then, you are probably going to take a tumble.

Jesus said it – if you're filled with pride in yourself, you're going to get a reality check. The girls you are pushing down as you push yourself up ... well, they may end up more important than you!

> "All those who exalts themselves will be humbled, and those who humble themselves will be exalted."
>
> Luke 14:11

Living It

Linda wants to be popular and she will do pretty much anything to make sure it happens. She spreads gossip about other girls. She told lies about a girl who is popular so that the girls in her class won't like her. She is not nice. What's going to happen?

The girls will figure out how selfish Linda is and eventually she won't have any friends. The girls she has been lying about will end up with more friends than Linda. It's the same lesson Jesus teaches ... think about how you treat others. Be kind. Be friendly. Encourage others to be the best people they can be.

Count on It

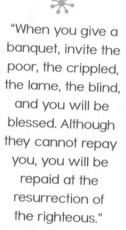

"When you give a banquet, invite the poor, the crippled, the lame, the blind, and you will be blessed. Although they cannot repay you, you will be repaid at the resurrection of the righteous."

Luke 14:13-14

Once again Jesus makes the point that the girl who follows Him does not give her attention only to those who are popular, powerful, wealthy, healthy or useful to her.

Pay attention to the people the world pushes aside. Help them. Be their friends. No, they can't pay you back for your kindness, but Jesus will pay you one day. Count on it.

Living It

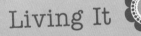

Lucy's birthday is coming up. She could throw a fancy party and invite her close friends, or she could have a simpler party and invite everyone in her class ... including the kids who never get invited to a party; the kids who don't really have any friends.

Yeah, that's what Lucy will do. Pay attention to those who don't receive much attention. It's the Jesus way.

Party On!

Think about it ... the moment you accepted Christ as your Savior a party broke out in heaven! A party because of you! That's how much Jesus loves you.

Every time a person turns to Jesus there is a celebration in heaven. He doesn't love one person more than another, but Jesus' desire is for all people to accept Him. He wants all people to be a part of His family.

> "I tell you that in the same way there will be more rejoicing in heaven over one sinner who repents than over ninety-nine righteous persons who do not need to repent."
>
> Luke 15:7

Living It

So what? Your party has already happened, right? So, why does this Scripture verse matter to you? Two reasons: One, stop and enjoy the thought that the angels and all the residents of heaven rejoiced because *you* joined the family.

Second, you have a role to play now in helping others find Jesus. You can have a part in someone else's party!

Celebrations

> "'My son,' the father said, 'you are always with me, and everything I have is yours. But we had to celebrate and be glad, because this brother of yours was dead and is alive again; he was lost and is found.'"
>
> Luke 15:31-32

Grace is when you get something you don't deserve. That's what the young boy called the Prodigal Son received – grace. When the boy who had wasted his father's money and hurt his father so badly came home, his father threw a party.

The older son, who had always been home, wasn't happy about this. He didn't want to be happy that his brother had come home. He couldn't rejoice with his father. He was too selfish.

Living It

Della is mad that her parents are throwing a party for her sister. "Erin gets everything. You like her better than me," Della complains. Of course that isn't true. She doesn't see the joy that her parents feel since Erin came home. Della's sister left home a few years ago and wanted nothing to do with them. She has asked for her parents' forgiveness and wants to be a part of the family again. It is just like the Prodigal Son and Della ... well, she's like the older brother. She can't stop thinking about herself enough to celebrate that her sister is back.

Priorities

There seems to be two main points that Jesus emphasizes over and over, among all the other things He teaches. Those two points are: Don't put a lot of importance on money and think about others before yourself.

The thing with money is either you have it or you don't. And, if you don't, then you want some. If you do, then you want more. Money is OK, but it should be shared with those who don't have enough, and getting it and keeping it should never be more important than God.

> "No one can serve two masters. Either you will hate the one and love the other, or you will be devoted to the one and despise the other. You cannot serve both God and money."
>
> Luke 16:13

Living It

Connie doesn't have money. She doesn't have a job. She's just a young girl, so the message of not serving two masters (God and money) doesn't seem to really apply to her. But her mindset is developing right now as to what her priorities will be as she grows up. Connie strives to keep her focus on putting the most value on her relationship with God and not letting money be too important to her. She is also careful to give some of whatever money she has back to God's work to help others. Good priorities.

Saying Thanks

> "Were not all ten cleansed? Where are the other nine?"
>
> Luke 17:17

Ten men who had leprosy called out to Jesus. Ten men asked Him to heal them. Ten men believed He could. Jesus did heal them and sent them to the priests to show that they had been healed.

One man came back to say thank you. Nine did not. Only one man praised God for the miracle of healing. Saying thank you is important. When Jesus does something for you, thank Him.

Living It

Talia prayed and prayed for a good friend who was very sick. "Dear God, please take away the disease in Brittany's body. Dear God, please heal her. Please." She prayed for Brittany day after day. God did heal her friend! Brittany is healthy again.

Talia remembers the story of the ten lepers and immediately thanks God for hearing her prayer. She thanks Him for the miraculous power that healed her sick friend and she praises Him for His love!

Heart Kingdom

The kingdom of God is not something you must look for far off in the future. Yes, there will be a day when Jesus comes to get His followers and take them to heaven.

But there is a kingdom of God right here and now. Because Jesus died for your sins, came back to life and now lives in your heart and because the Holy Spirit was given to you, the kingdom of God is right now – in you!

"The coming of the kingdom of God is not something that can be observed, nor will people say, 'Here it is' or 'There it is,' because the kingdom of God is in your midst."

Luke 17:20-21

Living It

Nora is a new person: a brand-new person. Oh sure, she has the same skin, hair and teeth. On the inside, however, Nora is new. She asked Jesus to come into her heart and be her Savior and immediately she knew that something was different.

As she lets Jesus take control of her thoughts and actions, she finds that she is becoming kinder. She is more concerned for other people. She has much more love for those around her. Her family has noticed it, too. God's kingdom is now in Nora's heart!

The Same Levels

"Let the little children come to Me, and do not hinder them, for the kingdom of God belongs to such as these. Truly I tell you, anyone who will not receive the kingdom of God like a little child will never enter it."

Luke 18:16-17

Once again Jesus points out that the strong and powerful people in the world are not really as important as they may think. It's important to receive God's kingdom like a child – with humility, trust and dependence on Jesus.

That's the only way to enter God's kingdom, because pride and power won't get you in.

Living it

Joanna thinks that it is so cool that even grown-ups need to come to Jesus like a child. Why? Because it puts everyone on the same level. No one is more important than anyone else.

Everyone bows down to Jesus and worships Him with faith, hope and love. That's the way it should be. He is in control and everyone bows to Him.

A Rich Man

A rich man came to Jesus and asked how to find eternal life. Jesus mentioned some commandments and the man said, "Yes, I've obeyed those." But there was one more thing Jesus wanted the man to do – get rid of everything he owned, everything he had worked so very hard to get.

Sell it all and not even keep the money, but give it to the poor! Once again, Jesus makes the point that it is important to take care of others. If they don't have bread and you do – share it with them!

> "You still lack one thing. Sell everything you have and give to the poor, and you will have treasure in heaven. Then come, follow Me."
>
> Luke 18:22

Living It

When Beth read the story of the rich man and what Jesus told Him to do, it stuck in her heart. She couldn't stop thinking about it. So, Beth went to her mom with an idea. "Mom, I've got tons more clothes than I can ever wear ... some I never wear.

Would you let me box up a bunch of my clothes and donate them to people who need them?" Her mom thought that was a good idea. Beth didn't donate junky, worn-out clothes. She sent good things, brand names, some that were brand-new and yes, some that she liked. Wow, she felt so good!

Giving All

"Truly I tell you," He said, "this poor widow has put in more than all the others. All these people gave their gifts out of their wealth; but she out of her poverty put in all she had to live on."

Luke 21:3-4

Jesus is so observant. He saw that while the rich man in the temple gave a generous gift, he actually gave just a little of the massive amount of money he had.

Then a poor widow who was also in the temple put two small coins in the offering. She gave more than the rich man because she gave all she had. She held nothing back from God.

Living It

What's the lesson from this story? Giving to God's work or to the poor is a good thing to do. But, if you give only out of your extra money, that doesn't really put a strain on you, does it?

If you give *all* you have or even give money that you may need, it shows that you are completely surrendered to God and that you trust Him to take care of you.

Living Water

You've probably heard the story of the Samaritan woman who met Jesus at a well. He asked for a drink of water and she responded rather curtly, because usually Jews wouldn't have anything to do with Samaritans.

The woman didn't understand who Jesus was. He told her that He could give her living water – water that never runs out because it is the life and joy of knowing Him.

> "If you knew the gift of God and who it is that asks you for a drink, you would have asked Him and He would have given you living water."
>
> John 4:10

Living It

What do you think the term *living water* means? Water is necessary for life ... all kinds of life, from the smallest plant to human beings. We all need water to survive. Jesus is called the Water of Life because when you ask Him into your heart, you are given a new life that will last for eternity.

The water necessary for the body to survive comes from outside. The water necessary for your spirit to survive comes from Jesus.

Teamwork

> ❋
> "Thus the saying 'One sows and another reaps' is true. I sent you to reap what you have not worked for. Others have done the hard work, and you have reaped the benefits of their labor."
> John 4:37-38

The work of God in this world is done through teamwork. You are a part of His team. That's pretty cool, isn't it? It's neat, because not every person has the same gift or talent.

Some people are really good at explaining the pathway to salvation, some are good at just being friends with people, some are good counselors, and some are good teachers. It takes everyone playing a part for one person to come to Jesus. Everyone is needed!

Living It

Jade knows she should be able to share her faith with her friends who do not know Jesus. But she gets tongue-tied when she tries. She is really good at just being friends with people, and showing them Jesus' love.

Jade is an important part of God's plan to share His love with those who don't know Him. She can be the friend and someone else will do the explaining. It takes a team!

Spiritual Food

Is Jesus saying that people who come to Him never have to eat or drink again?

No, He isn't talking about the physical bread and water that your body needs to survive. He is talking about the nourishment your soul needs to grow stronger in Him and to trust Him more and more. He is the food and water that will feed your spirit and give you eternal life.

> "I am the Bread of Life. Whoever comes to Me will never go hungry, and whoever believes in Me will never be thirsty."
> John 6:35

Living It

It is rather hard for Louisa to understand what Jesus is saying here. It's hard to see how her spirit needs to be fed. But as she thinks back over other Scripture verses that say whatever you put inside your heart and mind is what comes out of your mouth and actions, then it makes more sense.

If Jesus is her bread and water then the food she is feeding her heart is healthy and obedient to Him. That means her actions and words will be filled with His love!

Slavery

"Truly I tell you, everyone who sins is a slave to sin."

John 8:34

Can you eat just one potato chip? Or one piece of chocolate? Or whatever is your weakness? It's hard, isn't it, to stop with just one bite?

Sin is kind of like that. Once you start doing one little sin over and over, it becomes a habit and you do it all the time. Then, after a while that one sin isn't enough and you begin to do more. Sin is addictive so that you just can't get enough of whatever your weakness is.

Living It

Vanessa understands. She is a slave to sin ... to lying. She cannot stop lying. She knows with each lie she tells that she is digging a bigger pit to get out of, but she just can't help it. She lies to her friends, lies about her friends, lies to her parents and even tries lying to God. She is addicted to lying because she can't admit her mistakes and always wants to make herself look good.

The only way out of this circle of lying is to confess it to Jesus, repent and ask Him to give her the strength to stop.

The Good Shepherd

What is a shepherd's job? To watch out for his sheep, to take them to food and water and to protect them from harm.

Jesus is your good shepherd and He does these things for you. He is the Bread of Life and the Living Water to nourish your soul and protect you from Satan's tricks. Jesus laid down His life to protect you. He died for your sins and made it possible for you to personally know God and have eternal life with Him!

> "I am the Good Shepherd. The Good Shepherd lays down His life for the sheep."
>
> John 10:11

Living It

The part of this statement that speaks to Kelly is that Jesus protects her. She lives in a home where things get a little rough sometimes. Her dad has a bad temper and can get pretty harsh with the kids.

But Kelly has learned that when things get bad, she can call on Jesus for protection and care. He loves her and comforts her, no matter what is happening around her.

Knowing God

"If you really know Me, you will know My Father as well. From now on, you do know Him and have seen Him."

John 14:7

This must have been an amazing statement for the disciples to hear. Jesus was a living, breathing human being who they had traveled with and saw performing amazing miracles.

Now He tells them that by knowing Him they also know God! The only way they could truly know God was by knowing Jesus. That's true for you, also.

Jesus is the bridge to God and by getting to know Him, you learn to know God better.

Living It

When you think about it, this is an amazing statement and reality. You can actually know the Creator of the Universe, the powerful, magnificent, unchanging God. You can know Him!

The way you know Him is by learning to know Jesus. You learn to know Jesus by reading the Bible to learn His teachings and see how He treated people around Him. You will also see how He was always submitted to God and did His will. He honored God in all He did. A good lesson for you, too, right?

Friends with Jesus

Friendship is different from being a servant or even a student. Friends share news and they know what is going on in one another's lives. Friendship is an intimate relationship.

Jesus says you are His friend – if you obey Him. It's not hard because He doesn't ask you to do things without giving you His help to do them. He asks you to do things that make you a better person – kinder and more loving.

By doing what Jesus commands, you come into friendship with Him.

> "You are My friends if you do what I command."
> John 15:14

Living It

Victoria and Caroline are best friends. They talk every day and they share their dreams and hopes. They make each other laugh. They talk about their problems or things that make them sad. They know each other so well that they can finish each other's sentences. They can't imagine life without each other.

How cool would it be to have that kind of relationship with Jesus? How cool would it be to be good friends with Jesus? You can become that close by obeying His commands!

A Close-Knit Family

> "My prayer is not for them alone. I pray also for those who will believe in Me through their message, that all of them may be one, Father, just as You are in Me and I am in You. May they also be in us so that the world may believe that You have sent Me."
>
> John 17:20-21

Unity is important. All who call Jesus their Savior are in the same family.

Jesus prayed for unity among His followers. He didn't want fighting among them because that would take attention away from the message of Jesus' love.

He prayed that all of His followers would unite with one another and with Him and God. That's the best way for unbelievers to see the truth of His love.

Living It

Miranda and Josie are in the same class. They go to the same Bible study and the same church. They've been good friends for a long time, but just recently had a big fight. They aren't even speaking to each other now! But, they both realize that their fight creates a negative image of Jesus.

If two Christian girls can't solve their problems and get along with each other, what does that say to people who don't even know Jesus yet? So, the two girls sit down and talk out their problems and, just as Jesus prayed, unity is restored.

Heartbreaking Reality

This statement has so much in it. Soldiers had come to arrest Jesus and one of His followers pulled out a sword to defend Him.

He stopped His friend because He knew He was doing what God wanted Him to do. He knew it was going to be hard – He would be tortured and murdered – but it was God's plan for Him and because He was surrendered to God and because He loves you, He was willing to do it.

> "Put your sword away! Shall I not drink the cup the Father has given Me?"
>
> John 18:11

Living It

Barbara reads this verse and thinks about what may have been going through Jesus' heart and mind at that moment ... and her heart breaks. She realizes how very much He loves her.

Jesus was willing to face God's will for Him so that she would have the privilege of knowing God personally and the hope of eternal life. It's amazing. Jesus was completely surrendered to God.

Total Peace

> "Peace be with you!"
>
> John 20:26

Jesus often said, "Peace be with you." Even in the middle of terrible circumstances, such as after His own crucifixion, He came to His followers and said, "Peace be with you."

How could He expect them to have peace at a time like that? Because He wanted them to trust that He had a plan and that nothing that had happened surprised Him. If they could trust Him then they could have peace.

Living It

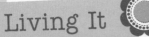

"Be at peace?" thought Mallory, "how on earth can I be at peace when the world seems to be falling apart? Everywhere I look there is a crisis or a problem. No one in my family is in a good place right now. There are wars and earthquakes and who knows what else. How can I have peace?"

Trust Jesus. None of the stuff that is happening is outside of His knowledge. He will see you through each day and you can trust Him to take care of you. Have peace.

Seeing Is Believing?

One of Jesus' disciples, Thomas, just couldn't believe that Jesus had actually come back to life after being murdered. He needed to see Jesus for himself. When he did, then he believed.

That's good, but Jesus gave a special blessing to the thousands of others throughout history who have not actually seen Him or touched Him, yet believe He is alive.

"Because you have seen Me, you have believed; blessed are those who have not seen and yet have believed."
John 20:29

Living It

It's easy to believe something that you can see with your eyes and touch with your hands. Believing that Jesus is alive takes faith because you can't physically see the man standing in front of you.

Faith is the basis for the Christian life. Jesus says you are blessed for believing and that blessing will give you eternal life with Him!

A Shepherd's Work

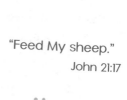

"Feed My sheep."
John 21:17

Three times Jesus asked Peter if he truly loved Him. Three times Peter replied, "You know I love You." Finally, Jesus told Peter to feed His sheep. What does that mean?

It means that Jesus wanted Peter to continue teaching what Jesus had taught him. He wanted Peter to help believers grow stronger in their faith in Jesus and to help do His work in the world.

Just as Jesus, the Good Shepherd, took care of His sheep, He wanted Peter to do the same.

Living It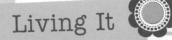

"So what?" Kendra thought. "I'm not a shepherd. I'm not a teacher. I'm just a girl, so what does 'feed my sheep' have to do with me?" Good question, Kendra!

Every believer has a role to play in the care of other Christians. By praying for others, Kendra is caring for them. By living out Jesus' commands, she is caring for others. Kendra does have a part in feeding the sheep, even if she doesn't realize it ... and so do you!

About the Author

Carolyn Larsen is an author, actress, and an experienced speaker with a God-given passion for ministering to women and children. She has spoken at conferences and retreats around the United States, Canada, and India. Carolyn has written over 40 books for children and adults. Her writing has won various awards, including the C. S. Lewis Silver Award. Carolyn lives in Glen Ellyn, Illinois, with her husband, Eric.

365 Days to
Knowing God for Girls

ISBN 978-1-77036-148-5

Written especially for girls who want to get to know God
better, this 365-day devotional will help them to focus their
thoughts on God as they learn more about His greatness.